NORTHERN CALIFORNIA

Also by Jack Newcombe:

The Fireside Book of Football
The Best of the Athletic Boys
A Christmas Treasury
In Search of Billy Cole
Six Days to Saturday

NORTHERN CALIFORNIA

A History and Guide

From Napa to Eureka

Jack Newcombe

Illustrations by Stan Skardinski

Random House · New York

Library of Congress Cataloging-in-Publication Data
Newcombe, Jack.
Northern California: a history and guide—from Napa to Eureka.
Includes index.
1. California, Northern—Description and travel—
'Guide-books. 2. California, Northern—History, Local.
I. Title.
F867.5.N684   1986   917.94'10453   86-10133
ISBN 0-394-72988-9

Manufactured in the United States of America
23456789
First Edition

CONTENTS

INTRODUCTION

The geographic appeal of California's North Coast and its
related ridges and valleys can come directly and easily enough
from a map of the region: the river-broadened valleys point as
vividly as fingers in north-south directions; the ranges pose a
challenging barrier to the ocean front; and the coast itself
marks a sharp, if irregular, definition between land and sea.
There are not the outer banks, penetrating bays or estuaries
one encounters along the East Coast. Northern California's
western border takes an abrupt stand against the vast Pacific.

But the unique appeals located here must be personally discovered. It is country of swift change—in climate, in terrain, in
the use that occupants make of the land. I have sat on Manchester Beach in mid-January against driftwood, being comfortably
warmed by the low sun and watching the winter surf slam
spectacularly against the shore. From the top of a flowered
Mendocino ridge in late spring, I have looked east toward the
Sierra where winter still was traced in broad white strokes. In
September, after a night of harmonizing coolness among
Sonoma vineyards, I have had to take refuge under a eucalyptus
to escape midday heat that only the deserts beyond Barstow
deserve. I have waited for the dense fog extending the night
around Humboldt Bay to lift and dramatically reveal a commercial marina shining with hope for the new day, however meager
the fishing hauls have become.

The surface of Northern California is quilted with contrasts:
the wild and preserved groves of the great redwoods, as primeval as forests can appear to us; the headland's grassy cover
flattened by the steady ocean wind; the rich seasonal presence
of rhododendron and poppy, of lilies and foothill lupine; the
trim brown grids of grape vines in early winter; scrub oak and
manzanita thriving on the steep flank of a ridge; the surprising
ridges themselves, which rise so quickly above planted fields

and the intermittent towns with their new, semiattached developments.

As a Vermonter, I have viewed Northern California with a mixture of familiarity and the astonishment that comes when confronted with the new. The two states have similar longitudinal shapes and physical characteristics of forested peaks and picturesque valleys. Vermont's western border, Lake Champlain, is hardly a drop in California's Pacific, but it provides the benefits—and hazards—of deep water, hard waves and winds. Perhaps my analogy stops here because there is no match in America for California's diversity or the choices it offers in recreation, road travel, light, weather or raw scenery.

I have often wondered how much the sight of the stunning country provoked the early Mexican explorers—who, as the first colonists, became *Los Californios*—or the American pioneers who made the long passage from the East and Midwest to claim the territory. And there were the Indians, the only occupants for hundreds of years, who surely spent their seasons working the land, fishing the rivers and coastal waters, and probably found little time to celebrate the beauty that surrounded them. They did, of course, offer thanks for what the land provided by blessing the early fruits of spring and by ceremonies that prepared for the vital acorn harvests in the fall.

As elsewhere, Northern California's Indian past seems to have been all but erased. True, it survives in historical society archives, in some museums, in influences on contemporary art (such as the ubiquitous craft of basketweaving), in the numbers of rancherias that remain populated by descendents of survivors of Indian wars and white man's diseases. Yet the Indian names remain: Arcata, Napa, the Mayacamas Mountains, Ukiah, Gualala, Petaluma. They blend pleasantly with the sounds of the place names that the Spanish-Mexicans left behind.

The most northern of the 21 missions formed in California by the padres of the New Spain, San Francisco Solano in Sonoma, was employing and converting Indians by 1823. Although the missions did constitute a first network of white outposts along the coastal frontier, it took the appearance of Mexican military leaders and an ambitious land-grant system to place Northern California under Mexican control, however briefly. Mariano Vallejo and Cayetano Juárez are the famous pioneer names— military men who controlled wide fiefdoms, granted to them by their government, and who parceled out land to cooperative American settlers. After California in 1825 became a territory of Mexico (which had just gained independence from Spain), they assumed the roles of leaders and protectors, roles the mission friars were not equipped to handle. Their presence discouraged the Russian fur traders from extending their bases farther south. By the time of the American takeover, these grantees were the large developers of crops and livestock.

Both Vallejo and Juárez were influential in the transformation of California following the Treaty of Guadalupe Hidalgo in February 1848, which led to California's admission to the Union. The Mexicans and the eastern adventurers and traders who had earlier answered the call to California were soon joined by the thousands who charged into the high valleys and mountains seeking gold and silver in the late 1840s. Many in this invasion eventually decided that mining prospects were very thin but that a living could be made in growing fruits and grains and in harvesting the thick forests.

The new population came via the long overland wagon routes and by the even-longer passage around Cape Horn. Sierra mining camps may have been built overnight, but it took longer to erect the lumber and fishing towns that dotted the Northern California coast and that stand today in their modern, modified shapes. There were no quick, mother lode fortunes to be made in the production of oak tanbark or railroad ties or lumber lengths, but there was employment in an industry with a future. (Unfortunately for the land itself, the demand for, and yield in, timber were so high that vast old-growth forests were quickly and heedlessly logged over.) The valleys, with their ocean-influenced climate, attracted immigrant farmers who learned that there were both self-sufficiency and profits to be had in the growing of vegetables, fruits, and nuts—and in extending the production of hops for the new breweries and of grapes for the new winemakers. California had approximately 200 wineries within the first four decades of statehood.

Northern California's Mexican- and American-made past is so close, compared with that of New England, that visitors feel as if they can reach out and touch it. The Victorian buildings in towns, the landmark wine cellars, the original health spas, the first community churches or schoolhouses have received but recent restoration or preservation status. Yesterday's log-hauling railroad that winds over the coastal ridge is today's popular sightseeing route; the showcase home of the nineteenth-century lumber baron is the brightly painted focus of tourists' cameras. Yet the strongest sense of the region's past comes from what was there when the early settlers arrived: the sweeping, uninhabited land of big trees, the eroded streambeds and low valleys and, always, the ocean.

My journeys through Northern California have encouraged me to retrace routes and revisit towns, places and parklands that have become favorites. But with each trip comes a reminder that the totally unfamiliar lies just around a sharp turn in the road or across the near ridge. California north of San Francisco is awesomely large and varied; the landscape of monotony lies elsewhere.

For the purposes of this book, I have confined the territory to Napa, Sonoma, Mendocino and parts of Lake and Humboldt counties. Drawing boundary lines, I am forced to omit the Point Reyes National Seashore and Tomales Bay in Marin County, which are rewarding starting places for any exploration of the northern coastline. My travels in Lake County have concentrated on the western or more populated Clear Lake area and do not include the large, empty national forests beyond. I chose

Eureka, surrounded by redwoods and the sea, as an appropriate
northernmost chapter. That decision leaves the reader to explore, with my encouragement, the Humboldt County roads
that hug the coast and lagoons en route to Oregon and those
that lead inland to the Klamath-Trinity river region.

I travel, as I hope everyone does, with a few unshakable
preferences and prejudices. I like old, wide-porch hotels; motels
without swimming pools; bars that invite fishermen's complaints; restaurants that face the sea; the look and feel of walking trails in early morning; smalltown parks where you can sit
and read the local weekly; beaches heavy with driftwood. I avoid
bed-and-breakfast inns because U.S. hosts have never mastered
the art of shabby gentility their English forerunners invented,
town festivals that last longer than one day, weekend brunches,
steak and seafood houses with truckstop-sized parking lots. I
can confirm a few more adverse opinions indigenous to Northern California: group wine-tastings, winery tours by the numbers, walnuts by the bagful, one-way streets in one-way towns.
And oh, yes, logging trucks.

My road guidance has come from a range of sources, as indicated by my acknowledgments, but I would recommend, in
addition to county maps, a few steady references for first-time
or regular visitors in Northern California. *The WPA Guide to
California, the Federal Writers' Project Guide to 1930s California,* offers a concise history of the state and town-by-town tours
that graphically describe the land fifty years ago and provide
exceedingly informative guidance today. There is, if anything,
an oversupply of available advice on wines, wineries and the
wine country; however, I wouldn't tour the vineyards without
The Pocket Encyclopedia of California Wines by Bob Thompson,
first published in 1980. The sometimes problem of leaving the
lovely, frustrating seaview Highway 1 and actually reaching the
ocean is best cleared by taking along *Coastal Access,* prepared
by the California Coastal Commission. This handbook not only

leads you down the path from bluff top to beach, it provides environmental information that makes the trip more meaningful.

The use of a town library or the resources of the local historical society (after a careful check of public hours) can enhance a journey. I have found those in Northern California communities to be most tolerant of, and helpful to, travelers. These small information centers are ideal goals in the midday valley heat or when a coastal fog has shut out the rest of the world. I am particularly grateful to the Mendocino County Historical Society branches in Ukiah and Willits, where its museum is located, for helping to educate me on the region's past.

There are in Northern California wide gaps between towns and places, thanks to the generosity of the land, but I have encountered a consistent willingness among the people to steer me in my chosen direction and offer local wisdom to broaden the way. Although I feel confident that routes taken—and suggested—will remain valid for time to come, restaurant and hotel rates vary and managements change. Local inquiry does help to lighten a traveler's load.

NAPA COUNTY

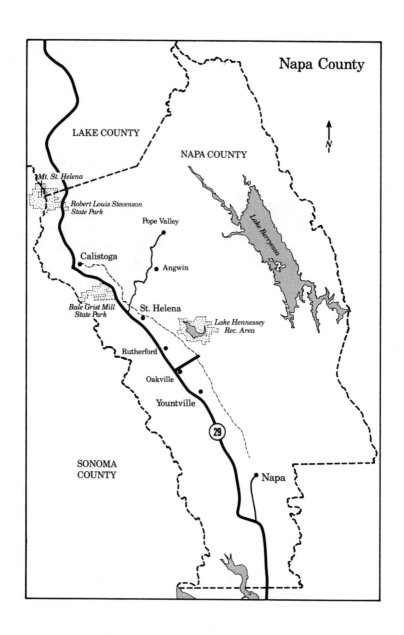

Consider San Francisco and Oakland as gateways to Northern
California, and the routes north swiftly set themselves. But the
getaways are often accompanied by the feeling that everyone is
going where you are. I have been bogged down by this midtraffic
dejection on Route 101, which leads across the Golden Gate
Bridge from San Francisco, and on I–80, which serves the
Alameda County side of the Bay from Oakland. But I later
learned that by shedding county boundaries, one by one, I gradu-
ally gained a certain freedom of the road. By the time I drove
past the ranchlands on the approach to the city of Sonoma or
caught sight of the arching Napa River Bridge below Napa, my
mood had decisively changed. Heading north in Northern Cali-
fornia does eventually become a buoyant way to go.

Napa City

T HE city of Napa offers few easy clues to its past. Of course,
its designation as the seat of justice for Napa County when
California achieved statehood in 1850 is evident in the grand
white courthouse whose spiraling cupola decorates the center of
town. The civic block is about all that keeps Napa from the
appearance of another lengthy suburban development-out-of-
nowhere. Approach the city from the south, past the municipal
golf course and Napa Valley College on the left and the entrance to the state mental hospital on the right, and one is on
the ubiquitous boulevard of auto sales, repairs and parts. Stay
on Soscol Avenue and search for the heart of the city, which
should be over there to the left somewhere, and you plunge into
the maze of one-ways, no-U-turns, left-on-arrow-only warnings

that lead to horn-honking frustration. On my first encounter with Napa several summers ago, I learned that the ultimate tourist folly was my attempt to find in-the-shade parking to avoid blistering my hands later on a steering wheel turned painfully hot by the noonday sun. The local shopkeepers, courthouse attendants and city hall office workers had taken the sun's August path into account hours before.

If there seems to be no Napa City today, traces of what it was as a bustling tannery town and navigational river port can be found with a little effort. Although the Napa River is now—except in a season of heavy rain—a narrow creek as it courses the middle of the valley and is more of a sluggish estuary as it approaches San Pablo Bay, it once was a major transport system. It was the reason that Nathan Coombs of the new state governing body laid out the town in 1848 at the head of the tidewater. Long before that, Nappa Indian tribes had built settlements along the banks and made use of its marine resources.

At the city's small River Vista Park, between 2nd and 3rd Streets, it does take a long reach of imagination to see the river as it was a century ago, lined with a half-dozen large wharves and ships prepared to carry grains, flour from local mills, wine barrels and hides south to Oakland and San Francisco. By the 1850s, regular ferry sevice was available between Soscol and San Francisco; with access to the Napa Valley Railroad, it became a popular tourist carrier for the valley.

The flow of produce and manufactured goods on the river continued into the 1920s, when the shift to roads and vehicles became general in the north. Napa was a commercial town on a tidal river but no longer a port of frequent call. Recently, only Kaiser Steel and Basalt Rock, two major employers located on the Napa-Vallejo Highway, have made much use of the waterway. There is a marina below the Imola Avenue Bridge, and the river can be observed the length of the John Kennedy Memorial Park adjacent to Napa Valley College and the municipal golf course.

Although it is hard to view the river as a once-prominent shipping lane, there remain two examples of the flourishing tannery business, begun in Napa in 1869, that sent great stacks of hides and leather materials downstream and to international ports. The pioneer tannery, Sawyer of Napa, still produces famous-label sheepskin coats and other products at its plant on Coombs Street—and visitors are welcome to see the venerable leathermakers at their trade. A few blocks away on South Coombs, near the entrance to the Wine Valley Lodge, the Calnap Tannery also operates near the river's edge.

Napa's most historic structure exists today as the Old Adobe Bar and Grille, where Soscol Avenue meets the Silverado Trail (Route 121) below the Fairgrounds. It is described as "California's second oldest adobe building" and was built by Cayetano Juárez, a Monterey-born Mexican army officer who had been sent to help General Mariano Vallejo deal with Indians at the Sonoma Mission. In 1837, Juárez received a grant, arranged by Vallejo, of two leagues (8,865 acres) east of the Napa River. Industrious and successful in getting Indians to work for him, Juárez built Rancho Tulocay into a wealthy source of livestock and crops. Twenty years after he became a major grantee, he donated 48 acres of land to the new town of Napa for the Tulocay Cemetery, which now fronts on Coombsville Road. By the time of his death in 1883, Juárez had become Napa's foremost resident.

To consider what once must have approached an arcadian life in the south end of the valley, a visitor might take advantage of 850-acre, community-sponsored Skyline Wilderness Park, east of Route 121 on Imola Avenue. The remnants of the stone fences Juárez built to protect his livestock from attacks by bears and other predators can be seen from hiking trails, and the chaparral and the meadow flowers were surely there when he was running his herds in the hills. The park includes picnic areas, a lake, and riding stables for those who enjoy traveling

Skyline Wilderness Park near downtown Napa includes 850 acres with hiking and equestrian trails cut through rolling hills.

as they did on Rancho Tulocay. More elaborate riding facilities are available at **Wild Horse Ranch** (Phone: 707–224–0727) on the extension of Coombsville Road that leads to Green Valley in neighboring Solano County.

For the nonequestrian, nonhiking visitor, there is the Napa option of taking a balloon flight for an unrivaled view of towns, vineyards, the valley and the hills that make it all possible. The balloons usually lift off shortly after sunrise while there is still night coolness in the air and the winds have not picked up velocity. The hot-air ballooning centers are Napa and Yountville; the cost of flights averages $125, with reservations necessary. (In Napa, Balloon Aviation of Napa Valley is located on Ornduff Street, near the 1st Street Exit on Highway 29. Phone: 707–252–7067.)

I discovered a hedonistic way to think about the Napa area's past while surrounded with modern luxury by visiting the **Silverado Country Club,** located to the northeast of the city off Monticello Road. The Silverado spreads its two 18-hole courses, designed by Robert Trent Jones, and 20 tennis courts over land once held by General Vallejo's brother Salvadore. By the 1870s, General John F. Miller Civil War veteran and California politician, had acquired 1,200 acres of the rancho and began constructing his own grand mansion on Milliken Creek, which flows from Atlas Peak 2,600 feet above the valley. More Italian-French than Spanish in style, the Miller home is now, after many expansions, the Silverado Clubhouse. General Miller's considerable living room, 84-feet long and 20-feet wide, is the club's lounge.

The Silverado is one of northern California's most extravagant golf and tennis resorts; on its rolling, manicured, creekside grounds are more than 250 guest accommodations, from studios to three-bedroom cottages. Spring and summer rates range from $145 to $335. Greens fees for condominium guests are $32 per round; tennis court fees are $12 per person. But even if you are not equipped with clubs or racket or a club member, the Silverado is a good choice for a self-indulgent lunch. Dodge the aggressive golf carts loading and unloading in the parking area and notice that the eucalyptus seem to have a richer resin smell and the patterned spray from the garden sprinklers gives the illusion of coolness even in the eye-blinking, 95° sunlight.

Hot-air balloons rise over Napa Valley vineyards carrying sightseers on early morning "champagne flights."

I began a midday interval at the Silverado with a drink at the long, modern, state-of-the-art bar in the lounge, wondering not what General Miller would think of the thickly cushioned stool I had slumped into, but what he did with all of the high-ceilinged spaciousness he required a century ago. Somehow, over the time it takes to sip a very dry martini, our needs perhaps had coincided.

The wood-paneled Royal Oak Room, overlooking the terrace and the 18th green on the south course, is the place for lunch. It has an open hardwood-charcoal (nonmesquite) grill and a reputation for excellent chops and steaks. I selected the Dungeness crab with avocado and melted Sonoma jack cheese ($8.95). The choice eliminates the possibility of ordering the popular appetizer "seafood on silver"—a galaxy of shrimp, crab and oyster on a knoll of ice. In keeping with the atmosphere, the wine list is long on quality. The Royal Oak is one of those rare country club rooms-with-view where the nongolfer can shut out the boasting voices of those who miraculously escaped double bogeys and enjoy the food—and, if one chooses, watch the intense middle-aged striving on the dark green lawns beyond the windows. A postlunch stroll around the club should include a study of the impressive old stone wall by the terrace, made smooth years ago by the seasonal thrusts of Milliken Creek. The original stonemasons placed planting urns between the stone panels, and flowers now grow there as they were intended to from the beginning. (Phone: 707–257–0200).

If you have neither time nor inclination to dine well at the Silverado, you might try to ease into the tiny parking lot in front of **Harry O' Shortal's Yard of Ale** on the corner of Lincoln Ave. and the Silverado Trail. It is a semifrantic purveyor of sandwiches, subs, burgers, tacos, chili and salads, with a wine and beer list almost, but not quite, a yard long. Some customers swear by the Sprite with cherry syrup and fresh lime. The Silverado Trail, leading up the east side of the valley, is mercifully free of roadside everything (except wineries). A takeout or a squeeze-in stop at the Yard of Ale is worth considering.

But if you are off and driving or biking the Silverado when hunger or thirst strikes, there is the coffee shop at the public Chimney Rock Golf Course just beyond Oak Knoll Avenue. Neither the pleasant nine-hole course nor the familiar-looking coffee shop intimidate strangers.

Yountville

Drive north from Napa on Highway 29, and if you are fortunate enough to be rolling free in moderate traffic you just might miss Yountville. The town is only a slight bend off the highway and is the location of the Veterans Home of California, spread institutionally at the base of the Mayacamas Mountains, which separate the Napa and Sonoma valleys. Turn right at the Veterans Home and you are in downtown Yountville.

For years, the town lived quietly with its connection to the Veterans Home and was content with a small reputation among wine country visitors. The hospital facility to the west was opened over a century ago for the disabled of the Mexican War; through the years, the surrounding ranchlands stretching to the Napa River and beyond were converted into vineyards. Residents are proud of the town's history as a pioneer settlement and its homey convenience at the entrance to Napa Valley. But now Yountville is committed to the tourist trade, its population has grown to over 3,000, and it is unmistakably becoming a mainstream row of lodges, motels, restaurants, shops and galleries. Even with its quickening commercial pace, Yountville still persuades me to stop for a meal; an overnight; a visit to the small wedge-shaped town park and a picnic lunch; or a trip along Yount Mill Road. Surrounded by a web of neatly maintained grape vines, Yountville manages to cling to its old image as an agrarian community.

At the north edge of town, Yount Mill Road, which loops

beneath tall eucalyptus trees toward the river before connecting with Highway 29, gives an appealing impression of the Yountville of yesterday. It also offers a historic connection: A simple stone marker at a turn in the road indicates the site of the 1836 blockhouse built by George C. Yount, "pioneer settler in Napa County." The original Kentucky-style structure, with its portholes for defense against raiding Indians, was replaced by a long adobe structure, also equipped with gun slots. Yount's gristmill and sawmill were located across the river. The marker describes Yount as "a trapper, rancher and miller" who died in the town of his name in 1865.

Yount was born in North Carolina in 1794 and was a farmer when he decided to accompany a trade caravan into the Southwest. At Taos, New Mexico Territory, he lived as a trapper with a group of mountain men, including Kit Carson. He followed William Wolfskill's trapping party in 1831 to the San Gabriel Mission in Southern California and, for a time, was active in the expanding sea otter trade. Like many who later followed his California quest, Yount's ambitions were basically agrarian, and these were strengthened by his stay at the Sonoma Mission just north of the great bay area. There he was influenced by the Mexican military-political commander of Alta California, General Mariano Vallejo. At the garrison, where Yount supervised the replacement of the thatched roof with protective shingles, he became enthusiastic about the rich valley lands and Vallejo's success with crops. His association with Vallejo resulted in a land grant from the Mexican government of 11,814 acres of what became Rancho Caymus at the base of Napa Valley. The North Carolina farmer-trapper qualified for the huge holding by agreeing to become a Catholic, a Mexican citizen, and promising to make structural improvements on the land. Yount eagerly began to develop the rancho with the support of Caymus Indians who lived in the valley and were quick to join him in his confrontations with the hostile Howell Mountain tribe.

When Yount was not dealing with "bad Indians," he was

supervising the planting and harvesting of his rich land and producing a modest amount of wine from the cuttings he brought from General Vallejo's vines. In 1844, he made 200 gallons of wine, hand-crushed, which were probably consumed by his family and the flow of friends and shelter seekers who arrived at the rancho. In the 1850s, Yount ordered a survey of the southern section of Rancho Caymus for a town he decided to call Sebastopol. A small community west of Santa Rosa also adopted the name of the Russian city on the Black Sea then under siege during the Crimean War. After Yount's death, the community he inspired became Yountville and California settled for one Sebastopol.

A drive or bike ride along Yount Mill Road or Yountville Cross Road (to the Silverado Trail) lets the imagination dwell on the success Yount had in the mid-nineteenth century in growing grapes and planting fruit orchards, in raising sheep and cattle and in running a flourmill. His achievements were challenged in the 1850s, as his success encouraged squatters to move into the valley after the large Mexican land grants, among them were the Caymus.

Today, tourists challenge the serenity of the vineyards and farmlands. In the Yountville Post Office, a clerk, who told me she had commuted to and from Napa for years, lamented the loss of the view of the vineyards across the road where a new motel complex had sprung up. "I do wish tourism had never happened to this valley," she said.

As a result of tourism, Yountville discovered in 1985 that it had acquired thousands of dollars in revenues in excess of its legal spending limit. Much of the money came from a boost in taxes on tourist rooms. **Vintage 1870,** a shopping center developed at the old Groezinger Winery on Washington Street— which operated from 1870 until 1954—attracts crowds to boutiques with names like The Wurst Place (sausages, smoked meats), The Grapes of Brass, The Highwayman (shoes, accessories). If you are turned off by the shopping mall cuteness, you

The former home and extended property of a Civil War general is now the site of the swank Silverado golf and tennis resort.

can still admire the splendid, hulking appearance of the winery building itself, which is on the national register of historic places.

Yountville accommodations offer variety: the tasteful, European-style bed & breakfast inns, the Bordeaux House and Burgandy House, on Washington Street; the new, dominating and pricey ($79 to $139) Vintage Motel with hot tubs all around; the Napa Valley Railway Inn, nine converted cabooses and rail cars on a siding behind the Yountville Depot; the Whistle Stop Bar and the Best Western International's Napa Valley Lodge at the north end of town.

The Railway Inn requires a certain fascination with trains, which I acquired easily enough as the son of a railroad man in New England. The cars are furnished with more imagination than most motel rooms. On a midwinter visit I chose "Railcar" No. 7 (off-season rate, $65; $85 to $95 on weekends in season). Within its lengthy 36-foot interior were easy chairs, couch, large brass bed, sizable tiled bath, three skylights and two bay windows—one facing the train platform and the other the vineyards. I sipped the complimentary wine and studied the stretch of vines, starkly trim in the low winter sunlight. No. 7 had been a refrigerator car in its rolling stock days and the thick walls provided insulation enough to let me ignore the heating and the air-conditioning units. With a little imagination, it became my "private varnish," as well appointed as the parlor cars of Jay Gould or any other rail baron. It never left Yountville, but it did take me on an overnight fantasy run. (Phone: 707–944–2000.)

For motel lodging of a superior sort, I would choose the **Napa Valley Lodge.** Its Spanish-style roof, shaded balconies and walkways and the swimming pool make it particularly inviting on a day of hot sun in the valley. I have stayed there in all seasons, with and without a working fireplace in the thick-walled rooms. The continental breakfast always offered a variety of fresh fruit. The Lodge is run by Best Western International, which also operates the ideally located Bodega Bay Lodge on the coast. The rates: $82 to $110, lower during off-season (Phone: 707–944–2468).

When motels are full and traffic off Highway 29 is at a peak, Yountville can hardly feed its hungry visitors, despite the increased number of restaurants. Among them, Le Chardonnay, in a compact brick building on Washington Street, offers generous, moderately expensive French dinners; nearby Mama Nina's provides, with less style and expense, Northern Italian cooking that attracts large family groups. Domaine Chandon, away from the town center and associated with the modern winery on California Street, has a traditional French menu. The two best restaurants in and near Yountville have developed reputations that lure a steady procession of repeat customers. Both are unpretentious in appearance, dependable in kitchen performance and moderate in price.

The Diner on lower Washington Street is, as the name suggests, a booth-and-counter eatery in a clean, well-lighted atmosphere. Local art hangs on the white walls and loyal customers choose from a breakfast/lunch menu served from 8:00 A.M.; dinner from 5:30 is predominantly Mexican fare. The heavy hitters may go for the huevos rancheros (basted eggs, jack and cheddar cheese, homemade chili sauce, corn tortillas, plus

grilled potatoes at $5.25) or the Santa Monica Special (a gener-
ous omlette with tortilla strips, plus the grilled potatoes at
$4.95). I was usually content—delighted—with fresh-squeezed
orange juice, poached eggs, fruit cup and toasted wheatberry
bread, which came to $3.20. Fruit in a cup—grapes, orange
slices, melon, apple, pomegranate—along with burgers, grilled
sandwiches and imaginative omlettes get a big play around
lunchtime. Wine and beer are available. The young staff works
hard and efficiently; the results are excellent. (Phone: 707–944–
2626.)

  Mustards Grill is just north of Yountville on Highway 29
and can be identified by the cluster of cars around a low, multiwindowed building. Afternoon or night, the parking lot at Mustards looks as if a convention is in progress. Convened there are
diners who swear by the dishes produced from a mesquite grill
and a wood-burning oven. Some favorites off the chalkboard:
thresher shark with red pepper and ginger butter, $8.95; Pacific
salmon with dill and shallot vinaigrette, $9.95; prawns with
black bean and ginger grilled in the shell, $10.95. On my last
visit, I wisely chose the special mesquite-grilled chicken breast
with avocado salsa and a glass of Groth Sauvignon Blanc from
the small winery on the nearby Oakville Crossroad. There is a
wine and espresso bar at the entrance; the tables in the rear and
in the pleasantly windowed front dining area are reasonably
spaced and forever busy. Dinner reservations in high tourist
season are not easy, but worth the effort. A late lunch offers a
better chance. If available, try the Napa Valley radicchio and
chickory with smoked duck breast and bacon from the appetiz-
ers, then experiment with the daily wine specials. The demands
of driving on nearby Highway 29 will ease away. (Phone: 707–
944–2424.)

St. Helena

The main wine road, Route 29, leads directly to and through St. Helena, surrounded by wineries both historic and boutique-new. The oldest operating winery in the valley, founded in 1861 by Charles Krug, is just north of town and so is Beringer Brothers, whose underground cellars were constructed before the turn of the century. The local population still reflects the heavy settlement of Germans and Italians who came to the wine business early.

The face that St. Helena presents to its visitors is well-preserved Victorian, with several expensive-looking outlets for provisions, wines, clothes and books on its main thoroughfare. The espresso cafes and restaurants seem reserved, and a comfortable old bar is difficult to find. At the south end of town, the high school stands impressively back from the highway and behind it are extensive playing fields and a local park.

St. Helena would seem to have little enough in common with bubbling Calistoga and vineyard-surrounded Yountville, but its beginning, as with the other valley communities, traces back to a major landholder who developed a thriving enterprise. Edward Bale, an English physician, came to the vicinity of St. Helena through an unlikely sequence of events. He was aboard a ship heading for California that ran aground off Monterey in 1837, an accident that encouraged Bale to accept a job as surgeon with the Mexican army. His marriage into the Vallejo family enabled him to acquire a sizable land grant in the upper Napa Valley. Dr. Bale continued his services with the army while attending to Rancho Carne Humana (human flesh) up north. The Bale-Vallejo in-law relationship was strained early when General Vallejo held back money from the physician's military pay because of a bad debt. Bale feuded openly with Captain Salvadore Vallejo and made the mistake of shooting at him on a Sonoma street, an attack that sent him to jail. When he was released, Bale sold a parcel of his rancho to begin the

construction of a flourmill on a small creek about three miles
north of the present town site. He also built a sawmill on the
Napa River. His decision was based on the rapid expansion of
wheat fields and cornfields in the valley and the growers' need
to convert the grain into flour. The Bale Grist Mill was built
solidly in 1846 of local Douglas fir and redwood; the original
grinding stones were quarried in the Mayacamas hills. The
waterwheel was 36 feet in diameter and weighed more than five
tons. The Bale Grist Mill became both a commercial and social
hub; within a decade, it had spurred the settlement down the
valley road. Bale did not live to see his gristmill in peak production. He died in 1849, age 38, after making a short run on the
goldfields.

The huge wooden wheel that powered the growth of the St.
Helena area can be seen in an excellent state-historic-park restoration. Located just off Route 29 north of St. Helena, the **Old
Bale Mill** is open to the public from 10:00 A.M. to 5:00 P.M. and
it displays trails to the former millpond system. The mill is a
mile and a half south of the entrance to Bothe-Napa Valley
State Park, open 8:00 A.M. until sundown, and is connected to
it by a walking trail. The park is a most convenient recovery site
for aggressive wine-tasters. The several picnic areas have large
tables, barbecues and water faucets. The trails are not demand-
ing. The swimming pool, a surprise in a Northern California
state park, is open summers. There are 50 family campsites that
must be reserved at least two weeks in advance during heavy-
use seasons (Phone: 707-942-4575).

On my last visit to the park, in early spring, I was much alone
among the redwoods, firs and madrone. On the mile-length Redwood Trail along Ritchey Creek, I walked in silence through the
ferns and Solomon's seal, wishing I could identify the flowers
emerging around the trees. The Coyote Peak Trail, which joins
the Redwood, requires some climbing but pays off with a fine
view of parkland and valley below. The park's easy accessibility
makes it a good day-use choice in the busy valley, particularly
in the spring and fall.

St. Helena presents an opportunity to examine the past—and to take refuge of a different sort—in its attractive, modern Public Library Center on Library Lane just off Main Street. It includes a semicircular library building and the **Silverado Museum,** which is devoted to the life and works of Robert Louis Stevenson. The museum (open noon to 4:00 P.M., closed Mondays and holidays) is small in size but large in its collection of Stevenson's letters and manuscripts, editions of his books, paintings and memorabilia—more than 7,500 items. As a reader of the more familiar works of Stevenson—and an early listener to readings from *A Child's Garden of Verses*—I was surprised by the sweep of his writings, which include poems, fables, history (the Samoan wars), essays, travel books, short stories and a half-dozen plays. The collection displays the copy of *A Child's Garden of Verses* that he gave his wife (I prefer Stevenson's original title, *Penny Whistles*); books from his library in Samoa; a redrawing of the map of a "treasure island" in 1750, which inspired the book; manuscript notes he made for *The Master of Ballantrae;* some of the lead soldiers he collected. It is surprising to see what a prolific writer Stevenson was after his marriage to Fanny Osbourne and his adventure at Silverado (see pp. 30–33), and that he produced so much of quality for young and adult readers before his sudden death at 44.

A personal celebration of Robert Louis Stevenson can be combined with some literary tasting at the Napa Valley Wine Library, housed in the public library next door to the museum. Wine book browsers, consumers in search of more expertise, viticulturists and student researchers imbibe the library's treasures in most appealing surroundings. One afternoon I sat at a table that offered a view of vineyards next to the library grounds and spent hours with old wine-label volumes. It was, in effect, a dry stroll through some of the older wine cellars of Northern California. They reflect the time when wine-conscious consumers were concerned about price and whether the wine was red, white or a fruity cordial. A label for "California Red Wine," bottled for the Southern Pacific Company, assured the purchaser that the wine was "Round, Mellow." Toscadero's "Invalid Port" was labeled "Very Choice Tawny." The Napa and Sonoma Wine Company of San Francisco, established in 1896, was satisfied with labels no more undecorative than those found on canned goods in grocery stores. But there was little need for creative labeling when, at the Los Angeles Ambassador Hotel, Beaulieu Riesling was $1.50 a bottle or a Paul Masson burgundy was $1.75. Restaurants and taverns considered it prestigious to present house labels: Freemark Abbey, for example, provided special labels that read "Selected and Bottled for The Spigot of Laguna Beach" on bottles of Claret, Zinfandel and Vin Rosé.

The pressure to turn creative, with labels that change about as dramatically as fall fashions, increased with the surge of new names in the field. Kenwood Vineyards delighted label collectors—and boosted sales—in the mid-1970s with a series of labels by California artists for their Cabernet Sauvignons. Kenwood was, of course, following at a modest level the style set by Phillippe de Rothschild of Mouton, whose label designers included Picasso, Chagall and Henry Moore, among others. Label looking gives one views of wineries never visited, of old cellars and hillside vineyards. And it reminds one that for all of his innovating and experimenting, Robert Mondavi long held to his conservative "RM" label for the vintage blends and that for years the same distinctive Indian "M" has represented the high quality of Mayacamas Vineyards on Mt. Veeder.

Label study is one way to spend time at the Napa Valley Wine Library, but one also might simply drop in to catch up on the *Wine Institute Bulletin* or another of the great number of periodicals that cover the industry. Inquire about the Wine Library's wine appreciation courses offered each spring. The library is normally open Tuesday through Saturday. (Phone: 707-963-5244).

Within a few blocks, St. Helena houses the sumptuous and mundane in eating possibilities—pizza-parlor swift to haute cuisine—requiring both advance planning and heavy cash funding. The latter is most famously represented by **Rose et Le Favour-Café Oriental,** a small restaurant on Main Street. Chef Bruce Le Favour operates the recently renovated restaurant whose menu combines his traditional French dishes with those of a Thai influence. The expensive prix fixe dinner has been changed to à la carte; luncheons are now served on weekends. (Phone: 707–963–1681).

The **Miramonte** and **La Belle Helene**, both in attractive settings on Railroad Avenue, boast ambitious French menus. A compromise for the visitor—and a good no-reservations luncheon choice—is the **St. George** on Charter Oak just off the south end of Main Street. Large and basically unpretentious—if you don't mind the ersatz oil lamps, the huge mirrors and paintings on the high brick walls—the restaurant offers sandwiches, salads, light Italian entrees at lunch. In seasonal weather, lunch is served on the wide patio of the reconstructed brick building. There is a cool, well-stocked bar just off the patio. Reservations for dinner in the spacious main dining room upstairs are needed. The "bistecca" (12-ounce New York cut) is $16.95; scampi $14.95. The Sunday champagne brunch fills the parking lot early. (Phone: 707–963–7930).

In the expensive/memorable dining category for the valley, the **Auberge du Soleil**, located on Rutherford Hill Road just off the Silverado Trail (south of Mt. St. Helena), has had a lofty reputation for several years. Early dining enthusiasts of the dramatically placed hillside restaurant say that kitchen changes have marred the original quality of the European-style dishes that showed inspired use of local produce. Napa Valley farm quail with game sauce, corn-fed hen with braised crayfish truffles and grilled salmon are on the menu along with local berries and other fruits of the season. The wine list is long and expensive. A dinner for two with drinks will exceed $100. I cannot compare the old and new Auberge du Soleil, which has expanded into a "resort" with rooms from $170, but I would recommend lunch on the umbrellaed terrace overlooking the valley, most particularly on an early autumn weekday afternoon (Phone: 707–963–1211).

The increase in restaurants of all culinary kinds in the St. Helena vicinity has even been exceeded by the proliferation of bed & breakfast accommodations. A lack of regulations made it relatively easy for owners of private homes to go into competition for overnight guests with the established inns, manors and villas that have been catering to the public for years. Real estate ads claim "ideal bed & breakfast" possibilities; bed & breakfast seminars ($250/couple) are held in winter weeks. The result has been a bewildering smorgasbord of shelter possibilities for the tourist who does want to reserve well ahead and avoid ringing the bell at Last Chance House on Friday night. Lacking previous experience or a solid recommendation from friends, the visitor is advised to contact the Napa Valley Bed & Breakfast Association (Phone: 707–257–1051) in Napa or the Bed & Breakfast Exchange (Phone: 707–963–7756) in St. Helena. There are other B & B associations that handle a select number of member inns.

For some time now I have been afflicted with a mild but unshakable case of B & B phobia. This travel disorder, which is closer to claustrophobia than agoraphobia, developed after a run of sorry experiences from too much chance taking at remote ranch houses and seaview "villas." I have never been enthusiastic about walking into a stranger's hallway, being greeted like a long-absent relative and quickly ushered to den or patio to "sit down, have a glass of wine and meet the other guests." One can do that in an unfamiliar saloon and keep the exit door in steady view. Nights are spent waiting for the shared bath to become quiet—free!—and wondering why the same *Reader's Digest Condensed Books* end up on uneven bedroom bookshelves. And the overly talkative breakfast produces soggy compliments for homemade rolls smothered with homemade jelly.

Shaded by giant eucalyptus trees, a ranch house suggests the pleasant rewards of growing grapes and fruit in the Alexander Valley.

I do know of an oasis where none of the common B & B symptoms appeared after revisiting, winter and spring. Located on Taplin Road just east of the Silverado Trail between crossroads Zinfandel Lane and Pope Street, it is the pleasant, private domain of Barbara Berglund. The **Farmhouse** is early-century mission-style, and its property runs close to the prosperous, rolling vineyards of Joseph Phelps. The accommodations—three double rooms—are in wings that offer privacy and the sounds heard through the open windows are rural-reassuring: a vehicle hurrying across the cattle grid down the small road, muted clanging of a sheep's bell from the hillside in the back, somewhere a dog's response. The antique iron bed in one of the Berglund daughters' rooms is towered with pillows and the books invite me into my own past. The sleeping is easy. Breakfast of fresh orange juice, melon and strawberries, rhubarb, muffins and coffee is surely what the long-ago traveler expected when innkeeping properly mixed hospitality with business. Rates at the Farmhouse are $75 and $95. No credit cards. (Phone: 707–944–8430.)

Calistoga

Any major agricultural valley needs a town at its head to serve as both gateway and geographic anchor. But few are crowned by a community quite like Calistoga, which is located in the northwest corner of Napa Valley at vineyards' edge and beneath the tall, naked shoulders of Mt. St. Helena. Calistoga was beckoning tourists long before the valley had acquired much of a wine-growing reputation. By a freak of geology, it began not as a market town for ranchers or silver miners still clinging to hopes in nearby hills, but as a health spa offering the misty benefits of its underground hot springs. The town got its identity from an enterprising Mormon developer who decided to combine the names of what he considered the best of all health-giving worlds—Northern California and Saratoga Springs in New York State. A planned nineteenth-century vacation and hot-mud-tub community, it has gone its own sprawling way in its ideal up-valley location. Two highways, 29 and 128, take the traveler right into town or swiftly around it. And the Silverado Trail provides a broad, pleasant approach on the east side of the valley.

Hydrotherapy, an "old faithful" geyser, a petrified forest just beyond one end of town, a dramatic mountain backdrop at the other, all that and the valley soil have helped build a community of 4,000 permanent residents and an economy that is basically tourism. The population within the town's 2.5 square miles is seasonally expanded by fieldworkers and, of course, the tourists who Sam Brannan had foremost in mind when he mapped out the town in 1859. He began with a "grand hotel" and 25 well-appointed guest cottages. Today, there are 7 spa-motels, 2 regular motels, 12 or more bed & breakfast inns, and a rebuilt hotel on the town's wide main street.

As founding fathers go, Samuel Brannan belonged with those who came west with a calling that somehow got lost among the blossoming commercial opportunities he found. Brannan, a 27-

year-old Irishman, was a leading Mormon activist in New York when he literally set his sails for California. In the newspaper he published for the Latter-day Saints, he had referred to California as "a portion of the new world, which God made choice above all others," and he eagerly accepted the mission of chartering a ship to carry 238 church members around Cape Horn to the western promised land. Before sailing in early February 1846, Brannan made a curious agreement with the shipping company that offered protection to the freedom-seeking religious sect in exchange for part of any land rights acquired by the church in California. The Brannan-led party landed safely six months later in San Francisco Bay, but Mormon leader Brigham Young dismissed the document Brannan signed as fraudulent.

The rough beginning of a new Mormon empire on the Pacific Coast included a store and printing shop run by Brannan. It soon came to pass that the major Mormon center, selected by Brigham Young and disputed by Brannan, was in the Great Salt Lake Valley far east beyond the mountains. In the gradual liquidation of Mormon holdings in California, Brannan managed to expand his own small commercial empire. He opened a store next to Sutter's Fort at the junction of the American and Sacramento rivers, a move that put him in a position to cash in on the gold rush without lifting a pick or a pan.

Brannan has received legendary credit for igniting the gold rush. One story has Sam walking the streets of San Francisco in early May 1848 with a small bottle of gold dust, bragging that it was "gold from the American River!" His printing press did spread the news of the discovery. Sharp business foresight enabled him to buy out his store partner for $50,000 and to spread his enterprises from the Bay Area to Sacramento. When Brigham Young informed him that it was time he shared his prosperity with fellow Mormons at Salt Lake, he refused. He was read out of the church, a censure that left him with a heavy burden of guilt but not without plans for the future.

When Brannan acquired 2,000 acres of valley land below Mt. St. Helena, he intended to build "the greatest resort spa in the west." What he accomplished was grand enough to attract folks all the way from San Francisco and to form the basis for a town that would grow around and above the vapors. Today, the Sharpsteen Museum on Washington Street offers tourists a romantic diorama look at Brannan's "Little Geysers and Hot Sulphur Springs," complete with hoop-skirted ladies playing croquet near the resort's large arboretum. The development included a one-mile trotting oval, a dance pavilion, a fish pond and a druidical grotto. Connected with the small museum is a cottage, with restored nineteenth-century interior, that displays the comfort offered spa guests at that time.

Brannan's own career did not long parallel the grandeur of the resort. He was accused of ruining pasturelands by letting his imported sheep run free; in a dispute over the ownership of a sawmill, he was shot and partially paralyzed by the wound. When Sam Brannan died in 1889 in a town north of San Diego, he had little to suggest that he was once considered the wealthiest man in the state.

Calistoga's early boom years saw the growth of a Chinatown near the Napa Valley Railroad Depot, where trains dropped off spa customers and carried away fruit and nuts from nearby farms. The Chinese community supplied fieldworkers, servants, gardeners and builders of the stone fences and bridges that are still prevalent in the valley. They dug winery tunnels and helped erect the Calistoga Silver Mine, which had an unprosperous run in the 1870s but gave the town of Silverado on Mt. St. Helena a reason for being. Menefee's *Sketch Book* comments that with the silver rush on the eastern side of the valley—a decade behind the gold rush—"every unemployed man from Soscol to Calistoga turned prospector. Blankets and bacon, beans and hard bread rose to a premium and the hills were lighted at night with hundreds of camp fires." But "the general disgust of claim-owners may be conceived when the formal certifications of assay were returned. Most specimens contained no silver at all and the very best only a trace."

However, there were some profits made in the region in the mining of quicksilver. In 1870–71, the phoenix Mining Company made $50,673 on 73,440 pounds of the mineral; the Redington Quicksilver Mine produced over 500,000 pounds for a few years, but the price never reached $1 per pound, and the demand for quicksilver soon declined.

When the free-for-all scramble for silver subsided in the hills, Calistoga concentrated on making use of its limitless supply of sulphur, steam and hot mud. A tourist guide of 1881 reported: "There is evidently some mysterious agency at work underground at Calistoga not quite comprehensible to visitors . . . when a man finds the ground under his feet to be hot and the waters issuing from it to be in the neighborhood of the boiling point, he cannot well help harboring the suspicion that the Diabulous Ipse is at work within perilous proximity, especially if the imagination is somewhat helped to the sinister conclusion by a prevailing and most Stygian odor."

Charles Nance was one who saw profit in the "mysterious agency," and he erected a bathhouse for his "sanitarium," which exists as a landmark spa at the northeast end of Lincoln Avenue. An early competitor on the Springs Grounds, the nearby Pacheteau Baths was the scene in 1928 of one of the more spectacular unnatural geysers in town. A local well-digger, drilling for Mrs. Pacheteau, had reached a subterranean distance of about 150 feet when, suddenly, his equipment was blown high in the air by a geyser force later estimated at 1,000 pounds per square foot. Immediate efforts to cap the hot eruption failed, and soon geyser watchers were arriving from all over Northern California. It took days of heroic pumping by the Calistoga Fire Department to cool the geyser enough so that workers could contain it. To locals it was a reminder that somewhere beneath their new pavements and buildings the "Diabulous Ipse" was quite capable of throwing its weight around.

A geyser still performs, approximately every 40 minutes, for tourists north of town, although it lacks the exciting disorderly conduct of the one that removed the Pacheteau Bath House a half century ago. Another tourist magnet, the **Petrified Forest**, is a short distance west (six miles from town) on Petrified Forest Road, which leads off Route 128 to Santa Rosa. It is a legacy of the volcanic action from Mt. St. Helena and contains the rock remains of trees that were encased in lava beds and protected from the elements for ages. It was "discovered" by a man named Charley Peterson—later known as Petrified Charley—who lived on the site with his niece. It is privately run as a tourist attraction and is not to be confused with, or compared to, Petrified Forest National Park in the Painted Desert of eastern Arizona.

For the stranger, Calistoga presents an easy, mostly north-south civic face, with a large portion of the shops, restaurants and several of the spas on Lincoln Avenue or a block away. At one end just beyond the small, tree-shaded library is the Calistoga Inn, the best restaurant and bar in town or for several miles. Down the block, the Vista Theatre shows Spanish-language films on weekends and is near the Las Brasas Restaurant, offering Mexican mesquite cooking. It and El Faro, across from the Calistoga Inn, demonstrate the rise in the Hispanic population—16%, compared with 82% white, in the 1980 census (the Chinese population was counted as zero). At the corner of Washington and Lincoln, the Silverado Restaurant opens its doors wide on the covered sidewalk for crowds of diners and drinkers. En route to the depot at the end of the next block, Val's Smokeshop offers shelves of magazines, newspapers, Calistoga Mineral Water, juices, California wines, liquor and a small selection of groceries if one is in a hurried, antisupermarket mood. Built in 1868, the railroad depot has been the victim of two major fires; it was most recently reconstructed in 1978 and now serves as a specialty shopping center and headquarters for the Calistoga Chamber of Commerce. It is the second oldest standing depot in the state. The last regularly scheduled passenger train pulled out in 1929.

The Calistoga Airpark is in the 1500 block of Lincoln Avenue and much soaring activity takes place on its airstrip. A look into the daylight sky above the hills often brings a glider into focus, its pilot taking advantage of the long-lasting soaring conditions. There are rentals and rides at the airport, but anyone interested in soaring to a record valley altitude will have to climb above 25,000 feet. For rubbernecking passengers, 5,000 feet offers quite a spectacle.

Lincoln Avenue is broad enough to invite walking both pavement sides. Across from the depot, the **Mount View Hotel** is deserving of a visit—or an overnight stay—as one of the few attractive full-service hotels in Napa County. It is on the site of the nineteenth-century European Hotel, a victim of the town's damaging 1910 fire. It was reopened in 1919 by Johnn Ghisolfo, Calistoga's enthusiastic mayor, and flourished for a time in mission revival style. The most recent renovation, in 1979, has resulted in an extravagant art deco appearance.

The brick Armstrong Building (1902) at the corner of Washington and the Oddfellows Building (1887) join the stone Stephens Bank building across the street as three of the town's most historic and durable structures. Cross the Napa River Bridge and turn up Cedar Street and you come to a prize Calistoga residence, the Judge Palmer House or "House of the Elms." It is not as imposing as the J. H. Francis Home on nearby Spring Street, which has served as residence and local hospital for the last 100 years. A stop at the ice cream parlor at Cedar and Lincoln might encourage one to walk to the Fairgrounds on Grant Street. A Napa County Fair happens there at the July Fourth holiday period; sprint car races are scheduled several times during the summer on the half-mile dirt track; high school football games are played on the racetrack's infield gridiron. Adjoining and sometimes intersecting the Fairgrounds is the nine-hole Mt. St. Helena golf course.

The historic H. J. Francis home built in Calistoga in 1878 was later converted into a local hospital.

To enjoy the best dining in Calistoga make reservations at the **Calistoga Inn**, which also offers bed & breakfast accommodations. A very civilized dining room with quiet ceiling fans invites one to the wine list and to a choice from the several fish entrees, which range from the steady fish stew ($10.50) to poached king salmon ($14.50). I experienced a memorable meal with two glasses of the house Chardonnay, the grilled coho salmon with almonds and a salad ($13.50). For the very hungry, there is usually a Napa Valley walnut pie available. The inn has a strong enough wine list and a bewildering selection of bottles of bottom-fermented lagers and top-fermented ales plus steam beer on draft. For an ale treat at the inviting bar with separate street entrance try Samuel Smith Pale from Tadcaster, England, and for a sturdy beer taste, the Hurlimann Stern Brau from Switzerland. (Phone: 707–942–4101.)

El Faro across Lincoln Avenue provides nonelaborate Mexican food in a building that once served as Calistoga's creamery. I found it a convenient source for tacos and Tecate beer, even for a take-out meal if you order and then take a stroll down the block. Another order-to-go choice is the tiny **Chicken Shack** on

Washington Street, which serves robust breakfasts to those who squeeze into the few tables. There are burgers, sandwiches, salads to take with you; a Chicken Shack breakfast is worth an early rising.

Beyond the center of town, where the Silverado Trail meets Route 29, before it twists toward Mt. St. Helena, **The Lord Derby Arms** presents an English pub appearance, complete with under-the-arbor tables outdoors. Potted shrimp, fish and chips, Cornish pastry, shepherd's pie and English and Irish beers and ales give the place an authentic taste. The fish and chips—Icelandic cod dipped in beer batter—are recommended. After an unlikely midday pub stop in wine country, one can be easily inspired to pull up to the Silverado Market, an open barn just up the road, for a supply of the local walnuts and a choosing among the plums, nectarines, oranges and apricots piled on the fruitstands.

For those who want to experience the full or partial treatment in "The Hot Springs of the West," there are several spa motels offering traditional and modern bathhouse therapies. All have mud and mineral baths, massage and blanket wrap, and some promote herbal facials, foot reflexology and acupressure. Treatment rates for "the works" at **Dr. Wilkinson's Hot Springs** is $35 (cheaper by the half dozen). At **Golden Haven** a mud bath with facial is $45. Nance's Hot Springs offers a volcanic ash mud bath with a half-hour massage for $32. In addition to conventional motel units, most spas offer kitchenettes and private Jacuzzis.

If you are not tempted to sink into a combination of volcanic ash and hot mineral water and simply require a night's rest, I would point you toward two economical choices: The **Mount View Hotel** has 25 double rooms, from $48 to $68, and more expensive suites. Even the smallest rooms are furnished with heavy 1930s dressers and nightstands, art deco bedframes, and the largest wastebaskets you may encounter on the road. All rooms have vintage celebrity names and an advance request

could put you in the Carole Lombard suite. A continental breakfast is included. Cocktails are served in the very art deco lounge.
Dinner at the Mount View is expensive by local standards.
(Phone: 707–942–6877.) The **Wardway** motel blends easily with
the residential surroundings at Pine and Myrtle Streets, two
blocks off Lincoln Avenue. It appears to be and is a moderate
and pleasant alternative to the more modern facilities in town.
It has been operated as a motel since the 1930s. I favored
a separate, spartan cabin at the rear of the motel with a kitchenette area ($30). It looked out over field and vineyard, and
early morning brought much bird sound through the open windows. (Phone: 707-942-6829.)

Bed & breakfast information in the Calistoga area is best
acquired through the Chamber of Commerce (Phone: 707–942–
6333). Rates are in the $65 to $85 range; some of the inns have
a resident masseuse.

Mt. St. Helena/Robert Louis Stevenson State Park

Calistoga spreads out on the valley floor 365 feet above sea level,
but only eight miles away, at the summit of Route 29, is the trail
leading to the 4,344-foot peak of Mt. St. Helena. This dominant volcanic dome stares down on Calistoga, the upper valley
and Northern California for miles around. From the top one
looks south to Mt. Diablo, guardian of San Francisco Bay;
northeast across the great Sacramento Valley to Mt. Las-
sen; and west to the surprisingly close Pacific. The mountain
rises in what has been designated **Robert Louis Stevenson
State Park** and although listed as undeveloped, it does include a parking area and a well-defined trail. Good hiking for
the most part, the Stevenson Memorial Trail is five miles to
the top and can be a challenge during the high sun of the day.
A Stevenson monument is located just over a mile from
the parking area. The twisting, sharply ascending road from

Calistoga, not to be attempted after prolonged wine-tasting, is an appropriate introduction to the alpine experience of the park.

The famous Scottish author's connection with this Northern California peak may come as a surprise to readers of *Treasure Island, The Strange Case of Dr. Jekyll and Mr. Hyde* or *The Master of Ballantrae*. But the mountainside served as a temporary—and highly romantic—home for him in 1880 following his marriage to American Fanny Osbourne. The couple spent their honeymoon in a deserted bunkhouse at the short-lived Silverado Mine; they also stayed for a time in Calistoga at what is now the Vermeil House on Washington Street. Stevenson was in his mid-twenties and a writer of travel books when he met and fell in love with Fanny Osbourne, ten years his senior. When she returned to California to obtain a divorce from the husband who had abandoned her, Stevenson determinedly followed, traveling ship steerage.

Stevenson's happy experiences on the wooded slope of Mt. St. Helena are related in a small book of sketches, *The Silverado Squatters* (1883). A combination of bucolic enthusiasm and personal history, it provides a delightful way to look at the landscape as Stevenson saw it over a century ago. (A paperback edition printed for the Silverado Museum in St. Helena is available at bookshops in Calistoga and St. Helena.) Stevenson became acquainted with indigenous trees and shrubs—the madrone, the manzanita, the buckeye, the redwood—and he paid the 50¢ entrance fee to view the phenomenon of the Petrified Forest. His well-to-do British background and his travels gave him an appreciation of European wines, and he explored the Napa Valley wine business "still in the experimental stage" and predicted, "The smack of Californian earth shall linger on the palate of your grandson." One of the vineyards he visited was owned by Jacob Schram and was the first hillside winery in the valley; it is now Schramsberg cellars, producer of excellent sparkling wines.

Stevenson had suffered from respiratory disease in Britain, and the need for more sun and drier air was one reason he and his forty-year-old bride chose the Silverado for an extended honeymoon. Although the mining town itself had been mostly carted away, the nearby Toll House Hotel was a regular stopping place for riders on the stage between Napa and Lake counties. Stevenson describes the first look he and Fanny had of their rent-free quarters: "Only in front the place was open like the proscenium of a theatre and we looked forth into a great realm of air, and down upon treetops and hilltops, and far and near on wild and varied country. The place still stood as on the day it was deserted . . . Fanny and I dashed at the house. It consisted of three rooms, and was so plastered against the hill that one room was right atop another."

The Stevensons' residence on these abandoned mineral grounds required logistical support via the Toll House; if it was awkwardly rustic, it was also constantly provocative. Stevenson was fascinated by the periodic "sea-fogs" that on some early mornings obliterated the land below: "Far away were hilltops like little islands. Nearer, a smoky surf beat about the foot of precipices and poured into all the coves of these rough mountains. The colour of that fog ocean was a thing never to be forgotten. For an instant, among the Hebrides and just about sundown, I have seen something like it on the sea itself. . . . Even in its gentlest moods the salt sea travails, moaning among the weeds or lisping on the sand; but the vast fog ocean lay in a trance of silence, nor did the sweet air of the morning tremble with a sound."

I am left envying Stevenson his unique experience in that unlikely summer place of years ago, in a house "everywhere so wrecked and shattered, the air came and went so freely, the sun found so many portholes, the golden outdoor glow shone in so many open chinks, that we enjoyed, at the same time, some of the comforts of a roof and much of the gaiety and brightness of al fresco life."

Each evening the Silverado squatters welcomed a brief push of air, "a lilliputian valley-wind," that signaled it was time to retire. The Stevensons' bedtime ritual included the carrying of an "unshielded taper" to their bunkhouse, and he speculated about the impact this light in the wilderness may have had at the time: "But the more he is alone with nature, the greater man and his doings bulk in the consideration of his fellow-men. Miles and miles away upon the opposite hilltops, if there were any hunter belated or any traveller who had lost his way, he must have stood, and watched and wondered, from the time the candle issued from the door of the assayer's office till it mounted the plank and disappeared again into the miners' dormitory."

Today's traveler can share some of Robert Louis Stevenson's wonder of that mountain environment by walking up the Memorial Trail, by driving to the high ridge on Route 29—or by reading his recollections of that honeymoon summer.

Napa Beyond the Valley

For every visitor intent on sampling Napa wineries, there is a motorist, usually a resident of the northern Bay Area, determined to spend a weekend or longer at Lake Berryessa, in Pope Valley or in Chiles Valley—all beyond the vineyard hills. Take Route 121 toward the Lake Berryessa Recreation Area, 25 miles northeast of Napa, and you find yourself in the unsteady hum of RV and boat-trailer traffic. The area is under the Bureau of Reclamation's control, and although there are shore resorts and housing developments with Century 21 Realty signs and shiny new red hydrants on suburban-wide streets, much of the 160-mile lakefront is open to the public. Boating, swimming, fishing are the games people play on this lengthy man-made stretch of water.

The names of the lake and valley come from Jose Jesus and Sisto Berryessa, who received an enormous, eight-league

(35,000-plus acres) grant in 1843. The land-rich Berryessas built a fine adobe home on Las Putah Rancho (Putah Creek feeds the lake from the north), and among the legends that grew up about the family is that of a famous brigand named Joaquin who was given refuge at the rancho. A Yankee bounty hunter is said to have approached the Berryessa headquarters and inquired noisily about the Mexican fugitive. Suddenly a man appeared and said, "I am Joaquin. Prepare to die." And without allowing time for even scant preparation he unloaded two pistols at the bounty hunter.

Chiles Valley, named for grantee Colonel J. B. Chiles, lies to the west of Lake Berryessa and can be reached by Route 128. A fast approach from the valley below is via the Rutherford Cross-road to the small Lake Hennessey Recreation Area, with its Conn damsite, and on to the Chiles and Pope Valley Road.

Pope Valley—William Pope was a grantee of two leagues in 1843—is a most winning place. It is best reached by taking Deer Park Road off the Silverado Trail above St. Helena, a road that climbs steeply to Angwin, home of Pacific Union College, which was founded by Seventh Day Adventists in 1882. The college and small surrounding village sit atop the crater of an inactive volcano, although there is little in the forested countryside to suggest such a geological past. The town of Pope Valley is another four miles to the northeast, and then the road wanders pleasantly through ranchlands to Aetna Springs, where a public nine-hole course is attractive enough to make you wish you played golf. The route crosses Pope Creek, another tributary to Lake Berryessa, and leads north on the Butts Canyon Road, the most scenic approach to Middletown, which, for the lack of a better civic stamp, is the gateway to Lake County. But it earned its name as the place halfway between Lower Lake and Calistoga on Route 29. The drive to and from Calistoga covers the wheel-turning, low-gear course between Mt. St. Helena and surrounding peaks.

Lake County/Clear Lake

In the highly literate and still cogent *WPA Guide to California,* Lake County is introduced as follows: "Into the wooded glens of hermit-like Lake County—never penetrated by a railroad—lead State 20 and 29. From the rocky hillsides gush mineral springs, and in the sheltered, oak-dappled valleys, clearings are green with bean vines on poles, pear and walnut orchards. The road hugs the shore of hill-encompassed Clear Lake, largest sheet of fresh water lying wholly within the State."

The description applies well today, except, perhaps, for "hermit-like." Lake County was, in 1985, noted as the fastest-growing of California's 58 counties, a result of the influx of retired people taking advantage of the high open country and of young people seeking jobs in the growing geothermal industry. Still, Lake County boasts trackless mountains, glens, orchards, a huge lake and now small wineries with developing reputations. It remains far down the state's county population list, with less than half of Napa's 101,000.

I have approached Clear Lake via Middletown by the alpine route from Calistoga and by the Butts Canyon Road from Pope Valley, which is my choice because it takes me through cattle country and bird activity around Detert Reservoir, which is fed by something called Bucksnort Creek. Middletown draws Seventh Day Adventist and United Methodist churchgoers and tourists who choose between Route 175—leading to Anderson Springs, Harbin Springs, Ettawa Springs, Loch Lomond and Boggs Mountain State Forest—and Route 29, which climbs more or less directly toward the lake. Take 29 past the newly sectioned town of Hidden Valley Lake, cattle and horse rangelands and the signs along the roadside: TV satellite sales, propane gas, RV sales, mobile home sales. Lower Lake Village, a crossroads about a mile and a half from the southern tip of Clear Lake, is a decision point: Route 29 runs close to the highly developed west side of the Lake; Route 53 merges with 20, which hugs the northeastern shore. Beyond Lucerne on Route 20 is the sometimes paved Bartlett Springs Road, which winds into the expansive Mendocino National Forest. At Lower Lake, I bought picnic supplies at Fuller's Superette and studied the names under "Returned Checks" writ large on the market window.

I was anxious to visit Kelseyville on Route 29 before exploring the busy bays and land points. Kelseyville has been called "Peartown" and "The Pear Capital of the World," but long before pears and walnuts became important cash crops in the vicinity, it was a remote rancho on which Salvador and Antonio Vallejo herded cattle. When, in 1847, they sold their holdings to a group headed by Benjamin Kelsey, the basis for a town with a name was set. In the shadow of Mt. Konocti (4,200 feet), which rises beside Clear Lake, Kelsey and his partner Stone built an adobe, marked now by a monument on the edge of town. Their harsh treatment of Indian workers—this was Pomo territory before the white invasion—resulted in decisive local justice: The Indians killed Kelsey and Stone in 1849. Kelsey Creek now flows into Kelseyville, and there near the waterfront is the Big Valley Indian Rancheria—a reminder of the site before orchards were planted.

The orderly spaced walnut trees and the gnarled-looking pear trees reach across the hillsides around Kelseyville, and at some ranch entrances are signs indicating that a walnut dryer is available. I walked Kelseyville's slow-paced main shopping street and stopped at a large brick cafe for a beer. As in most smalltown saloons, it was easy to take a quick economic survey. The man from Vallejo had purchased nine lakefront lots for $10,500 each a few years ago and said he'd been offered $50,000. "But I'll wait—that's my retirement. My place in Vallejo is smaller than the one I've got here just for weekends. How do you figure that!" He keeps a 19-foot inboard and a small outboard. "Everyone here's got at least that," he said. He fishes for crappie, largemouth bass and catfish and wishes the lake was deep and cool enough for trout.

A half century ago Clear Lake was rich in fish, birds, water plants, insects. Power boats did not then dominate the 43,000 acres of freshwater, about 25 miles from end to end. But in the 1940s, it was decided to attack the chronic gnat problem by putting insecticides in the lake. The gnats were controlled but the fish suffered, and the lively bird population of western grebe was greatly reduced. Gradually, the lake was reclaimed and the loonlike grebe are seen in abundance, feeding and raising their young.

Kelseyville gives entrance to **Clear Lake State Park** on Dorn Bay, with nature trails, picknicking, campgrounds and boat-ramp use for modest fees. It is one of the few easy-access areas on the lower section of the lake. The uneven, hilly shore-line below Mt. Konocti is terraced with houses and cottages, and bulldozers are steadily at work flattening out new building sites. For a totally undeveloped waterfront—and some fishing for stocked trout—you have to go to **Indian Valley Reservoir**, with 4,000 acres of water impounded in 1975. It is 10 miles northeast of Clear Lake. Access roads are few.

An extravagant, pleasurable way to view or use Clear Lake is to stay at the **Konocti Harbor Inn**, reachable by Route 29 or the Soda Bay Road. The Konocti is popular for its tennis, golf and boating/fishing package plans and its facilities are within

On twenty-five-mile-long Clear Lake, a busy summer boating and fishing scene, a tourist boat makes its daily run out of Konocti Harbor.

reasonable reach of the 240 rooms scattered in separate units around the inn. I arrived when off-season rates were in effect, and an upstairs (lakeview) room cost $48. Rates climbed to $112 for a deluxe apartment or beach cottage. Summer season prices are considerably higher and inquiries should be made about the many package possibilities (Phone: 707–279–4281).

The Konocti Harbor Inn Marina, with adjacent swimming pools, is the large centerpiece of the family resort. Boat rentals range from $6 an hour for paddleboats and rowboats to $75 (a two-hour minimum) for 460-horsepower ski boats. The all-purpose, multiservice marina is open year-round, but off-season hours, Labor Day to Memorial Day, are much reduced.

I was there on winter days of sun and strong, lake-ruffling winds and chose the protection of the balcony off my room to a choppy tour of the bay. In the evening, both the lounge and dining room at the inn were sparsely attended with the result that the service from the young staff was definitely eager. Such are the advantages of attending a large resort when most guests are at work or in school.

Behind the Konocti Harbor Inn's prominent trademark totem poles and the familiar use of the Indian name in the area lies a legend passed along generations ago by the lake-dwelling Pomos. It tells about the wrath of the great chief Konocti after he learns of the request by rival chief Kahbel for the hand of Konocti's daughter Lupiyomo. Konocti challenges his enemy to a duel and the two chiefs hurl boulders at each other across The Narrows until Kahbel is killed. Konocti, mortally wounded, falls back to form the mountain by the lake that bears his name. In despair, Lupiyomo throws herself into the waters and is drowned. It is said that surface bubbles have marked the spot ever since.

The county seat, Lakeport, is just off Route 29 above Kelseyville. It looks over the widest stretch of the lake, about eight miles. The city has free boat-launching ramps at its convenient lakeside park and the congregation of cars, motorcycles and boat trailers can make for a slow passage through town. Lake County's fast growing pains are indicated in the weekly *Clear Lake Observer,* which gives considerable space to the logs from the sheriff's office and the police department. Speeding vehicles, barking dogs, window vandalism, domestic contention and petty theft seem to punctuate the good lakeside life. At **Vista Point** in Lakeport, one can get a quick fix on the way the area appeared before human intervention began. The roadside ecological viewing area was funded by the California Environmental Protection Fund through the sale of personalized license plates in 1973, as authorized by Governor Reagan. The viewing area (there were 12 in the state at the time) has maps and tables describing Clear Lake geology. The basin was formed during mountain building of 10 million years ago. The size of the body of water was gradually reduced as Cache Creek, an outlet at the south end, "stole" water and carried it uncertainly into the Sacramento River. The viewing location provides a fine panorama, and the comprehensible information on the ecology is worth reviewing en route to or when leaving Lakeport.

The area's climate and soil, which have given rise to the generous production of nuts and fruits, have also encouraged a return to the planting of vineyards, begun a century ago and then abandoned. **Konocti Cellars**, with its first crush in 1979, is midway between Kelseyville and Lakeport and is the county's leader in planned cases. **Lower Lake Winery**, outside the village of Lower Lake, earlier became the first bonded winery in the area since Prohibition. **Kendall-Jackson** on Highland Springs Road south of Lakeport has a picnic area set, appropriately enough, in a walnut grove above the vineyards. Lake County offers no challenge to Napa, Sonoma or Mendocino counties as a producer of wines, but it does like to boast of its own new labels.

The northern approach to or exit from Clear Lake is via Routes 29 and 20, a broadening highway in Mendocino County. The way leads past the Blue Lakes, Upper and Lower, formed at the base of Cow Mountain (3,858 feet). Upper Blue Lake offers good, deep fishing spots; it is stocked with trout and home to largemouth bass. Fishermen can find camping facilities at small resorts around the forested lake.

At the Blue Lake Motel the middle-aged barmaid gestured toward the dark water beyond the windows: "They say they've never found the bottom some places in the lake." (The higher the hills around a lake, the deeper the mystery of the waters.) She wore a heavy sweater as protection against the wind that slipped under the windows and said that her summers were spent working for the forest service as a fire warden at a station near Boonville in Mendocino County. The job combination—a sometimes-busy lakefront bar and the isolated mountain look-out—suited her just fine. Each spring she looked forward to seeing or hearing her neighbors around the fire-watch station —a split-eared doe, a few bobcats and wild pigs in the canyon below.

The Blue Lakes are in the northern part of the state's Cow Mountain recreation lands, more than 50,000 acres of the Mayacamas range separating Lake and Mendocino counties. The wildlife population includes wild pig, bear, coyote, black-tailed deer and small game, but only at the southern end of the hunting area is there direct road approach. The nonhunting motorist can be easily convinced that there is an abundance of wild game in the Cow Mountain forests simply by driving the scenic highway (Route 20) over the grade to Lake Mendocino and Ukiah.

Napa Wine Country

America's most famous grape-growing valley, narrowed by high ridges east and west and only some 30 miles in length, can be toured, wine-tasted and shopped in a day or so. But to begin to appreciate the wineries, old and new, and what they produce,

and to savor this most favorable environment, one's acquaintance should extend through all seasons and a harvest or more.
It can rain hard in the valley in winter, the fog can chill and
blind, a surprise spring frost can mean crop damage, the summer sun can sear unshaded ground or it can gently turn an
afternoon into a blissful passage. The vines grow heavy with
reassurance as the crush approaches and within a short period
they become stark cemetery rows with the beauty of infinity in
their closely trimmed branches. Wine country is much more
than the sum—and quality—of its yearly production. It is as
lovely as a cultivated land can be.

I became aware of this a few years ago on a fall afternoon
when I stood on a hill above the Silverado Trail and watched the
sunlight retreat from one vineyard after another. The permanent sprinklers and wind machines stood a tall, silent watch.
Smudge pots were so many punctuation points. I thought of the
harmony of other planted fields: corn rows marching up a hillside in Vermont, the sway of windblown wheat at the edge of
a Missouri town, the steady procession of walnut groves and
apple orchards—the fascinating geometry of things carefully
planted. Here the vineyards, laid out with considerations for
mechanical harvesting, have an encouraging preciseness all
their own.

It may have been that clear appeal that led me to visit the
small winery called **Villa Mt. Eden** near the junction of the
Silverado Trail and the Oakville Cross Road. Orderly sections
of the vineyard are visible from either the Silverado or the
crossroad, and the winery itself is seen as a few white, tile-
roofed buildings sitting low and far back among trees. The narrow entrance road runs through grape plants to a compound
that seems too small for tours, too functional to allow time for
visitors. (Villa Mt. Eden will arrange tours; the unpretentious
wine-tasting area is compatible with the modest-size ranch
facilities.)

Villa Mt. Eden is inclined to let its estate-bottled wines and its reputation for winning awards speak for the winery and does not attempt to compete with the showcase cellars not far up the road. On each visit since the first, three years ago, I have welcomed the familiar farmyard ambience of Villa Mt. Eden, although the teal blue finish on the edges of buildings does give them a distinctive, nonagricultural look. The color is there on the water tower and on the label, too, a Sebastian Titus drawing of a corner of the courtyard. The greenish blue color of the common river duck serves most agreeably as a barn trim or a wine bottle adornment.

The winery's annual production from a little over 80 acres is in the 18,000-case range, which places it in the small category by Napa Valley standards. This is Cabernet Sauvignon soil, and Cabernets, Chardonnays and Chenin Blancs are Villa Mt. Eden's concentration. This is half the wine variety of recent years, and it is the chosen direction of young winemaker Mike McGrath, who came to work for owner James McWilliams in time for the 1982 crush. McWilliams, an investment capital businessman in San Francisco, bought Villa Mt. Eden in 1972 when, he said, "things were moving in this field. It all appealed. It was in the right viticultural region. We liked the house that came with the winery. I liked the neat compound around the loading area." His wife, the former Anne Giannini, is responsible for the soft teal blue trademark of Villa Mt. Eden.

The label reads "Established 1881," which means that the winery—or at least the grape-growing ground—belongs to the viticultural history of the region. The 1880s saw real expansion of the young industry in Napa Valley. In 1980, Beringer Brothers had a capacity of 145,000 gallons, Groezinger 275,000, Charles Krug 280,000. Vineyardist Jacob Schram was producing 20,000 gallons. The *St. Helena Star* reported that a decade later there were 200 wineries in the region, although it did not differentiate between those of sizable capacity and the farm families who were squeezing grapes for personal consumption.

A grower named George C. Meyers—the name is inconsist-

The compact winery compound of Villa Mt. Eden, established in 1881 in Oakville, combines old barn buildings and modern technology.

ently spelled—apparently had 5,000 vines at or near the present Villa Mt. Eden site in 1881. A later survey by the California Board of Viticultural Commissioners indicated that the production was in Riesling and Zinfandel wines.

In 1886, the *Star* referred to "George S. Meyer of the Mount Eden Vineyard" and mentioned his bumper corn crop. The wine production was reported to be 52,000 gallons, more than enough to require a winery building on the property, once part of George Yount's Caymus Rancho. In 1887, Mt. Eden's rented acreage was 108—"this year yielding a fine crop." At that time, a fine or not-so-fine crop did not usually go into bottles at the winery. It was transported to San Francisco for bulk use, where wine merchants could water it down before it was shipped for sale.

By 1913, Mt. Eden Winery had been acquired by Nick Fangiani, one of the growing number of Italians who were influencing valley winemaking. In 1937, the *Directory of American Wineries* listed Fangiani's bulk sales at 100,000 gallons and the wine type as "dry."

In the modern era, Villa Mt. Eden passed through some fallow periods until 1970 when all acres were replanted. The next production came four years later, after McWilliams acquired the winery. He began modernizing the buildings and entered into a slowly rising production curve, knowing that the staged growth meant he would pass through nonprofitable times at the beginning. "If you want to make a little fortune in wine," he jokes, "start with a big winery."

McWilliams stays involved in the major decision making, and he and his wife, an enthusiastic gardener, spend weekends in the attractive 1930s house with a guest cottage and entertaining area attached. The day-to-day responsibilities belong to wine-maker Mike McGrath, a 1978 graduate of the country's leading viticultural school, University of California at Davis. McGrath has two assistants (more during the crush), and there is, of course, seasonal help. The job of running a winery, even one that stretches for 80-odd acres, all within view, takes 12 months' devotion to the subject. As one winemaker put it, "You get but one vintage a year and so you treat it like a child, before and after birth."

Villa Mt. Eden is an estate-bottled winery in the true sense: All the grapes used are grown on the property and the wine is fermented, aged and bottled within the small compound. The winery has its own destemmer and field crusher, a fairly rare and expensive device in the valley. It is practical because of the close proximity of the vineyards, but it can be a problem if the weather is hot during the crush. McGrath would prefer to crush under more controlled conditions. A fine 1985 Chardonnay yield and cool weather enabled McGrath and his crew to finish pick-ing by late morning and to use the crusher at the winery.

I caught up with the young winemaker on a typical January workday. He was hoping to do some strip spraying if the wind died down; he was also overseeing the critical pruning opera-tion. I was surprised to learn how much wood is removed—up to 90%. "You cut the cane back to where there are ten buds on a cane," he explained. "The canes get tied down to prevent wood damage." He showed me a vine in which the two-wire system was used for protection. "There are," he said, "three basic types of pruning. Head pruning; cordon pruning, the most prevalent because of the action on the grapes during machine harvesting; and cane pruning. An experienced worker can prune about a half an acre a day." The workers were also involved in other January chores such as tying and stick replacement.

He took me inside the chilly wine cellar where he has a small office. The white wines were in the two-week process of cold stabilization in tanks; the reds, having gone through fermentation, were ready for the oak barrels piled high around us. McGrath said that viticulture was not the prime reason he went to UC Davis from a San Diego high school. He was given a track scholarship and became a standout in the steeplechase and 5,000 meters. "At one time I even thought of dentistry," he said, "but in the sorting-out process I first studied brewing and then switched." He liked the new challenge that winemaking presented and the possibility it offered of improving the product year after year. He apprenticed under Miljenko (Mike) Grgich, the Croatian wizard of Chardonnay wines, at Grgich Hills in Rutherford. He went to Adelaide, Australia, where he received training in the difficult art of making a good wine from less than ideal grapes.

The job of chief winemaker has reduced McGrath's physical outlets, but he appreciates the range of activity in which he is involved at Villa Mt. Eden. "I wanted to be in on all phases of winemaking, not specialize," he said, "and here I can do it all, from vine and lab analysis to the harvest to bottling—even go out and help market the wine."

Four months later I interrupted McGrath during barrel-cleaning time, when he was preparing 240 barrels for the whites and 240 for the reds before the crush. He was dressed in shorts for the track season, but he said that despite the fine days he still had to keep a frost watch. Winds, cold and the rains had made it a difficult few months for growth. But the growth was there, the very tiny green clusters of grapes that would determine the future vintage.

McGrath showed me the pride of the winery, the two-acre section at the front of the main building where the fruit is grown for the limited Cabernet Reserve lots. The grapes here develop in a soil that is better drained than that of the other Cabernet plantings, and they have a more earthy, eucalyptus-like flavor. (Yes, eucalyptus trees are an enhancing part of the scene.) He said that the critical factor in growing these grapes was the well-drained soil. Villa Mt. Eden is in the lower part of Region II of Napa Valley's wine country and its contributing factors include warm temperatures and a gravelly soil. (The valley is divided into three general growing regions, from the cool-foggy Carneros area near the Bay north to Calistoga.)

Villa Mt. Eden's Cabernet Reserve receives longer aging in newer oak casks. The 1980 Reserve, a select, expensive (about $25–$30) choice for those who favor a hearty Cabernet, is what the premium red grape of California and its careful production at a small estate-bottled winery is all about. It came, appropriately enough, a full century after the first Mt. Eden winemaker chose this rewarding ground. (Phone: 707–944–2414.)

Villa Mt. Eden fits into the small, quality category of Napa Valley wineries, a judgment that, even as a visitor with no certain knowledge of the industry, I can make with confidence. But bewilderment sets in when I consider the entire roster of Napa Valley wineries—more than 125 in number, varying from cottage cellars with a few hundred cases produced each year to the household-name giants that have become subsidiaries in U.S. business empires. The growth of the winery crowd in Napa Valley is the result, in part, of a decision made by the Napa County Board of Supervisors nearly 20 years ago to avoid the urban sprawl that afflicted counties to the south. An agricultural preserve was established, enabling the extension of vineyards but restricting the subdivision of land. A change in the preserve agreement, a series of bad harvests or a drop in America's already modest wine-drinking habits (far below the per capita consumption of several European countries) could bring a different look to the narrow valley.

Wine tours, like wine, should depend on individual tastes. My own special selections of wineries visited do not reveal a fresh fruity nose or excellence in structure, nor do they have cheery overtones. They will not likely improve with age. They might best be described as slightly out of balance, with some raw oak flavors and, I hope, a good crisp finish.

Fortunately, Napa Valley's retail outlets, bookstores, motels and inns are all stocked with maps and guides which allow the visitor a choice of tasting and touring destinations. I would not make a trip to any wine district without *The Pocket Encyclopedia of California Wines* by Bob Thompson (Simon & Schuster). It may not make you an instant wine expert, but it will supply you with enough information to reduce the fear of getting totally lost in the vineyards. *The Wine Spectator,* twice-monthly, is directed to "people serious about wine." Its annual *Wine Maps* is a useful general guide to wineries, restaurants and lodging in California growing regions. *Napa Valley Wine Tour* (published by the Wine Appreciation Guild) has abundant maps, details on selected wineries and dining and lodging advice.

I have made Napa Valley winery visits from Vallejo to the south, from Lake County to the northeast and by crossing the ridge from Sonoma County to the west via Dry Creek Road and the Oakville Grade. The valley is easily accessible, although approaching it over the Mayacamas Mountains does limit the choice of routes. A planned visit to two or, perhaps, three wineries in a day is far preferable to a marathon tour of every beckoning building-with-visitor-parking along Route 29. The following short list reads, geographically, south to north, and starts on the Silverado Trail—the route I habitually take from Napa and the only way to go if you are traveling by bicycle. (Note that tasting hours at most wineries are 10:00 A.M. to 4:00 or 5:00 P.M. The larger wineries offer regularly scheduled or self-conducted tours; many of the small wineries give tours by appointment only (or not at all).

. . .

In the southern Napa Valley, Clos du Val's modern winery facility, opened in 1974, is visible from the Silverado Trail.

Clos du Val Wine Company As the Silverado Trail stretches into the widening south end of the valley and passes the Chimney Rock public golf course, a white, low-profiled building set well back to the right off the highway marks a French winemaker's presence in the region. Clos du Val is the creation of Bernard Portet, son of Château Lafite's winemaker. The young Frenchman chose what is known as the Stag's Leap viticultural region, which slopes toward the westerly sun, to plant his vineyard in 1972. He has gained a reputation for Cabernets that follow the French Medoc tradition and result in a smooth, less alcoholic, less expensive wine. Clos du Val is a low-key, well-integrated winery and a good introduction to the wine road ahead. (Phone: 707–252–6711.)

Stag's Leap Wine Cellars Located close to the Silverado but shadowed by heavy oak trees, this winery takes its name from the prominent Stag's Leap palisade to the east. Winemaker Warren Winiarski has an unlikely background as a sometimes lecturer in political science at the University of Chicago. He did take a two-year cram course in the art of winemaking at Robert Mondavi's before building his own reputation for well-balanced Cabernet Sauvignons and Merlots from grapes grown at vineyards just south of the winery. Stag's Leap Wine Cellars—sometimes confused with the smaller Stag's Leap Winery to the north, which is not open to the public—has retail sales in its handsome winery residence. Appointments must be made for a tour (Phone: 707–944–2020).

It is convenient to use the Silverado Trail, or what was sometimes called the Old Back Road, despite its reputation as the quick way to the silver mines, to reach wineries on busy Route 29. Oak Knoll Avenue, south of Clos du Val, or the Yountville Crossroad, north of Stag's Leap, will lead you to the following two wineries.

Trefethen This family-owned winery, built in the 1880s, produces its wines from a 600-acre vineyard close to Oak Knoll Avenue at the northern edge of the city of Napa. Managed by John Trefethen, it had its first crush in 1974, and the concentration since has been on producing wines from grapes grown on the family-owned land nearby (Phone: 707–255–7700).

Domaine Chandon Although it does not catch the eye as you reach Yountville on 29, this new, architectually impressive winery attracts crowds of visitors to its location on California Drive. An overseas offspring of the Möet-Hennessy empire, it quickly became the major sparkling wine producer in the valley after a 100,000-case capacity winery was constructed in the mid-1970s. The popularity of the *méthode champenoise* blends of Chardonnay and Pinot Blanc, the attraction of the winery complex and the attached restaurant, with dramatic outdoor seating in warm seasons, accounts for the high visitor attendance. (Phone: 707–944–2892 for restaurant reservations; 707–944–2280 for winery information.)

From Yountville to Oakville on 29, there are unbroken vineyards, right and left, but to explore those that reach and seem to disappear into the hills and ridges of the Mayacamas Mountains you need to turn left on the Oakville Grade. It leads out of the valley and into different wine country. The Oakville Grade spins over the top of the ridge and into Sonoma County. Signs at the start warn, "Trucks Not Recommended." The first time I used it, east to west, I was distracted by a side road at the foot of the hill that led to what looked like a splendid old estate residence fronted by vineyards. It proved to be a Carmelite monastery, and the immediate property has served as such for the last 30 years. It was too late for Sunday Mass and too early for Vespers and Benediction at 4:30. I stopped for a while in the small side chapel, or prayer room, which was full of early-after-noon sunlight but without other wayfarers or worshipers. A rewarding place, I decided, to pause before mingling again with traffic on 29 or making the steep climb up the Oakville Grade.

Far Niente   A road nearly opposite the one leading to the monastery runs south through pristine vineyards to the closed, iron-gate entrance of this winery building, which dates to 1885 and was a famous source in pre-Prohibition years. It is open only to the trade and by appointment, but my curiosity about the history of the place led to an arranged visit. The building, set against the quick rise of the Mayacamas, is a fascination, and the relatively young winery operation started in 1979 by Oklahoman Gil Nickel specializes in estate-bottled Chardon-nay, with planned growth in Cabernet Sauvignon. Far Niente, the name on the front of the stone building, was what John Benson called his farm and wine cellar in the 1880s. The Italian is a near equivalent of *sans souci,* without care. Much concern by Hamden McIntyre, who also designed the original wineries at Inglenook and Trefethen, went into the imposing structure, which has been expensively renovated by Gil Nickel and his brother and partner John.

The building, crowned with a multiwindowed cupola that serves as office space, contains fermenting tanks, barrel rooms and cellars on the lower levels and offices and conference and

Far Niente's wine-producing history began in 1885 and its restored stone building with original cellars is a Napa Valley landmark.

residential rooms above. One is struck by the size of the oak tables, the width of the fireplaces and the varnished oak spiral staircase that rises to the office cupola. From the outside, the vine-covered building, with its bridge entrance leading to the reception area, looms not so much as a historic preservation, but as a grand old winery given long-delayed, post-Prohibition life by optimistic new winemakers. (Phone: 707–944–2861 for the possibility of participating in a scheduled visit.)

Vichon As the Oakville Grade makes its first serious ascent, the small parking area of this new winery is located to the left, overlooking the level vineyards of the valley. Vichon's history reaches only to 1980, when its enterprising management group began an unusual blending of Sauvignon Blanc and Semillon. The result of fermentation in French oak puncheons and *sur lie* aging is light, white Chevrignon, a table wine that has developed a loyal clientele. (Phone: 707–944–2811.)

Vose Vineyards For an alpine vineyard experience, one

must take a road less traveled off the Oakville Grade. Turn left
on the well-marked Mt. Veeder Road, drive a mile and a half to
4,035 Mt. Veeder and follow the winding dirt road to Vose,
which is approximately 2,000 feet above the valley. When I first
located the winery, the young woman in the small retail sales
room said, "And how did you hear about us?" Vose does not
attract many visitors off the crowded wine road below, but it is
worth seeking out as one of the most picturesque mountain
valley vineyards. The Vose family began clearing the alpine
forests for grape growing in the early 1970s, and the stones from
the 120 planted acres are in evidence in the winery construction
and in the network of farm fences. Winemaker Hamilton Vose
produces a variety of wines, including Chardonnay, Cabernet,
Zinfandel and Zinblanca, the fruity "popcorn wine." Vose is
self-contained, and everything from laboratory work to final
bottling is done in house. The retail sales room and picnic area
are open daily; inquiries should be made for group visits (Phone:
707–944–2254).

Mayacamas   The Mt. Veeder Road that runs south along the
ridge connects with the one-lane Lokaya Road. Turn right on
Lokaya and note the "Please Drive Slowly" sign and the an-
nouncement of Mayacamas Vineyards, where visitors are welcome by appointment only. I arrived one cool spring afternoon
without calling ahead; however, there was little visible activity
and I was rewarded with a look at the facility and the selection
of a 1982 Chardonnay. The name of the vineyard comes from the
mountains that frame Napa County's western border, and it is
Indian in origin. The Indian expression *Mayacoma* (howl of the
mountain lion) and the word Indians used to indicate a direc-
tional marker are sometimes cited as the source for Mayacamas. It does have a lovely sound, and the winery has kept a
distinct Indian-designed lion-decorated M on its label for years.
(I saw a 1953 white Pinot Mayacamas label at the St. Helena
library that looked identical to the one on my bottle of Chardonnay.)

The winery was built in 1889 by a German immigrant who produced red and white table wines and ran a small distillery. Like other late-nineteenth-century cellars, it was abandoned for a period and then renovated in the 1940s. Present owners Robert and Elinor Travers took over the winery in 1968. Bob Travers circulates a lively and informative occasional newsletter that reflects a winemaker's concerns about weathers and vintages: "Our vintage parade was rudely interrupted by a half inch of rain on the morning of August 30 but commenced again two days later, no harm done. . . . The 1983 vintage of Mayacamas Sauvignon Blanc was harvested the last week of September. Autumn that year was very dry (reminiscent of some wineletters) so picking interruptions were infrequent. Again, time will improve these bottles and we recommend 1986 to 1988 consumption of this wine. . . . Vintage 1973 has always suffered in reputation due to being sandwiched between the famous 1974 and the notorious 1972. However, when fully aged and in its prime our 1973 Cabernet Sauvignon may well turn out to be the best vintage of the decade for us. When will this happen? Not soon. We recommend drinking it in the 1990s for it should be at or near its best for most of that decade."

For an appointment and directions to this outstanding winery on the slopes of Mt. Veeder, call 707–224–4030.

Mt. Veeder Winery Another small, uphill winery, this one is located south of Mayacamas on the Mt. Veeder Road. Twenty acres were cleared in the 1960s for a vineyard that has produced distinctive Cabernet Sauvignons. Visits by appointment (Phone: 707–224–4039).

Mondavi The name stays at the head of the major leagues of winemaking in Napa Valley—or any other region in California —with its modern facility in Oakville that fits the image of Robert Mondavi. Even wine buffs who consider the label too ubiquitous, the buses arriving for daily tours too many and the basic red and white table wines too familiar, admit that Mondavi is a stop to make on the wine road and that the proprietor is a man much admired and his methods much copied in the industry. The Mondavi complex itself is an architectural triumph: a low Spanish ranch-style building with a graceful arch and a stark white campanile set against the Mayacamas hills.

In his informal, entertaining biography, *Robert Mondavi of the Napa Valley,* British author Cyril Ray describes this wine magnate's boyhood as the son of an Italian grocer and saloonkeeper who moved from a mining town in Minnesota to Lodi, California, when times turned tough during Prohibition. There Cesare Mondavi bought and sold grapes for whatever purpose buyers around the country had for them. It was a legitimate way to roll up profits before the repeal of the Eighteenth Amendment. One of four children, Robert studied at Stanford and following graduation went into the family business at Sunnyhill Winery, where his father was the major partner. When Cesare bought the idle Charles Krug winery in 1943, Robert became general manager. A family feud split the Mondavis and finally resulted in a much-publicized 1976 court case. Brother Peter Mondavi took control of Krug and Robert took a settlement. The first vintage under the Mondavi label in Oakville came in 1966, with the facility barely finished. Now in his early seventies, Robert Mondavi has turned over much of the ongoing operation to oldest son Michael, president and director of planning; son Tim, who handles production; and daughter Marcia, in charge of sales in the East. This family wine business is an employer of more than 200 people. Inquire about continuing art exhibits and scheduled concerts (Phone: 707-963-9611).

Beaulieu Vineyard Approaching Rutherford, the wineries flash by on the St. Helena Highway with welcome signs but no instantly familiar names until Beaulieu appears, standing close to the road and the rail link, across from the Rutherford Fire Department. Beaulieu staked out its claim here at the turn of the century when Georges de Latour arrived from France and

A vintage winery and a famous label, Beaulieu Vineyard was founded by Georges de Latour who defined it "a beautiful place."

decided that this was the place to grow grapes, develop a winery. Beaulieu, with all the traffic flow, may not suggest "beautiful place" anymore, but it has a proven place in the wine history of the region and its influence on wine buying is still prominent in the United States.

Bob Mondavi told Cyril Ray that when he first came to the Napa Valley in the 1920s to learn the wine business, "I bowed my head every time a BV (Beaulieu Vineyard) or Beringer Brothers or any of the other great firms' trucks went by."

Beaulieu may not command the respect it had in post-Prohibition times and through the 1960s because of its devotion to volume, but it still gets top credit for its Cabernet Sauvignon, Georges de Latour Private Reserve. In the 1930s, winemaker André Tchelistcheff, a Russian trained in France, developed a Cabernet tradition that has served this large winery very well. Beaulieu can boast that the best Cabernet Sauvignon soil— sandy and loose—and climate is within a six-mile radius of the crossroad on Route 29 where it is located.

Beaulieu's commercial success may be understood by the

manner in which its president, Legh Knowles, talks about the winery and California wines in general. Knowles is an an enthusiast but hardly a dilettante. A framed quote in BV's modern tasting and retail sales section puts the executive's attitude in perspective: *Customer:* "Do your wines have prismatic luminescence?" *Knowles:* "Would you mind repeating that in English?"

Knowles uses such plain putdowns of wine pedantry to encourage the drinking of wine for taste and enjoyment. I sat with him in a restaurant in St. Helena and shared a bottle of BV's Gamay Beaujolais, which went down most agreeably with whatever it was I had for lunch. Knowles said, "If I hear a wine steward say that the wine to drink with the *poulet Rochambeau* is such and such and I really want a simple Chardonnay, I order the Chardonnay." He suggested that the only infallible taste test for wine drinkers is: "If it tastes good, it's a good wine. If it tastes great, it's a great wine. But if it tastes fantastic, then you have discovered a fantastic wine."

Knowles has been in the business of promoting BV and the drinking of California wines for 24 years. He began his vocational training working for Ernest and Julio Gallo and wrote their first sales manual in 1961. It was at his urging that Cornell University's hotel management department first offered a wine course for students in 1952. But his background is in the big-band dance ballrooms of America, not its vineyards. At age 15, Knowles went on the road with the original Glenn Miller band as a trumpet player and later served in that section with Charlie Spivak.

"I think the two greatest thrills in my life," he said, "were the night we opened to that huge crowd in the Paramount in New York and when the curtain parted we were playing 'Moonlight Serenade.' It still sends goose pimples, just the memory of it! The other was being offered and accepting the job here at BV."

Knowles has seen small wineries grow up all around Beaulieu, an expansion that has not been matched by wine consumption in this country. "The new winemakers come in and work hard and don't make a profit. If the owner doesn't need to make a profit, then it's a good business." For BV it's still a very good business.

He reached for the glass of Gamay Beaujolais. "I think we've been forcing the allure," he said. "There is too much angular tasting." And he demonstrated by taking large, critical sniffs of the glass. "All that's necessary is to pour the wine, roll it, sniff it—and then drink it!"

The Beaulieu complex includes separate tasting and sales areas, a bar and a wine cellar. Lunch is served at patio tables in season. Daily tours, phone: 707-963-2411.

Inglenook A first visit to this historic winery a few vintages ago left me with the impression that it was a vivid example of an old wine cellar with surrounding vineyards that had gone agribusiness while still managing to maintain some of its original owner's charm. The approach avenue, a straight and impressive half mile, ends in a shopping-mall-size parking lot. Within the stately winery building, the piped-in music is bassoon and strings, the sales room offers oak wine racks for $89.95 and hand-crafted French oak casks for $350. At the large tasting bar an Inglenook representative explains, "Your taste buds are cleaner in the morning, therefore . . ." A taster from a wine tour bus group says, "This is a 1918 Chenin Blanc, really?" And the tasting barman says, politely, "No, I said 1980."

Inglenook has vineyard roots that, figuratively, go back to the previous century when Finnish sea captain Gustave Niebaum set idealistic goals for his new winery in Rutherford: "I have no wish to make any money out of my vineyard by producing a large quantity of wine at a cheap moderate price. I am going to make a California wine if it can be made, that will be sought for by connoisseurs and will command as high a price as the famous French, German and Spanish wines, and I am prepared to spend all the money needed to accomplish that result." According to the *San Francisco Examiner,* April 6, 1890, Captain Niebaum

The imposing headquarters of Inglenook are located among vineyards that were first planted in the 1880s by a former Finnish sea captain.

believed that the trick was no trick. "Grow the right kind of grapes on suitable soil, pick it when it is fully ripe, see that it is handled with scrupulous cleanliness and properly fermented, and you have an article that has no need of the skill of the cellarmaster."

About that time, Captain Niebaum was selling his wired, sealed, Table Claret Zinfandel 1884, guaranteed with the Pure Wine Stamp of California, for $4 a case of a dozen home-bottled quarts.

Inglenook tours, which cover old terrain and new winemaking methods, are scheduled daily (Phone: 707–963–7184).

Grgich Hills Set among the giants on the St. Helena Highway, a short distance north of Inglenook, this small gem of a winery pulls me back each year—if only to admire the ribbons and awards and sip a little Chardonnay in the small tasting room. The winery is the result of a partnership of vineyardist Austin Hills, of the coffee family, and Mike Grgich, a winemaker who previously had made a reputation for himself and for Château Montelena. (His 1973 Montelena Chardonnay was a surprise international winner in Paris 10 years ago.)

Grgich (try Gur-gich for pronunciation) was born into a large Croatian family in Yugoslavia in 1923 and was stomping grapes at the age of three at vineyards owned by his father. He began his viticultural education in California in the late 1950s: at Souverain, Christian Brothers, Beaulieu (as a chemist for André Tchelistcheff), Mondavi (where he admired Robert Mondavi's instinctive wine-promoting ability) and at Château Montelena (where he gained the reputation as a shaper of superior Chardonnays). At his own cellars in Rutherford, Grgich has done what he pledged he would do—produce Chardonnays, Rieslings and Zinfandels of varietal distinction and avoid the commercial quantity of his neighbors. On my last visit, after a year away, the one change I noticed was that the parking lot finally had been paved and a visitor did not have to worry about truck ruts. (Phone: 707-963-2784.)

Conn Creek   Back to the Silverado Trail via the Rutherford Cross Road, which bends into east-bound Route 128, and a recommended stop at a winery named after the creek that comes tumbling down, in season, from Angwin and into Lake Hennessey and beyond. Without a charming winery building, Conn Creek wins awards and praise from wine buyers who have identified the high quality of its Cabernet Sauvignon. (Phone: 707-963-5133.)

Rutherford Hill Winery   Take the Rutherford Hill Road off the Silverado and pass Auberge du Soleil to the quick end at this 10-year-old winery with a profile all its own. Haybarn in shape, it is all of weathered wood and designed to fit into the tree-lined hillside setting. The picnic area is shaded, the view is a small but splendid slice of the valley floor. Rutherford Hill produces its own wines under the guidance of Phil Baxter; the grapes and management support come from the long-established Freemark Abbey. (Phone: 707-963-9694.)

Napa Creek Winery   A decided contrast to the modern conception of Rutherford Hill, this small winery on the Silverado above Zinfandel Lane is located in a stolid, one-time meat-packing plant—ideal, the owners decided, for the production of a maximum of 15,000 cases a year. Jack and Judy Schulze, graduates of the University of Kentucky, came like pioneers of old from Ohio to make use of California's year-round growing conditions. Enter the old, cold meat-packing building and you know you are in a family-developed winery and not a bottling factory. Daily tasting hours; no appointment required. (Phone: 707–963–9456.)

Heitz Cellars   If you decide on a brief boutique winery circuit, this one, with a tasting and sales facility on the St. Helena Highway (near Zinfandel Lane) and with vineyards and cellar on Taplin Road to the east, is a good choice. Phelps, Stag's Leap, Chateau Montelena and Villa Mt. Eden (see above) also fit into the general "boutique" category—small, high-quality producers that have been developed with ample private funding. Winemaker Joe Heitz apprenticed at Gallo in the 1950s and learned the techniques of other wineries before placing name and label on his own carefully cultivated wines. He says that Heitz Cellars sometimes is referred to as wine hoarders rather than sellers, pointing to the care given to release time. Prices are high, vintage dates important at Heitz. The 1973, Martha's Vineyard Cabernet Sauvignon is approximately $650 a case; the 1976 Bella Oak Cabernet about $540. Heitz does offer some moderately priced 1981 and 1982 Chardonnays. For Cabernet devotees, Heitz is a visiting must. (Phone: 707–963–3542.)

Except for brief stops, I have avoided three of the best-known place names on the wine road in the St. Helena vicinity. I never actually made it to **Spring Mountain Vineyards**. There were too many people along the approach, snapping pictures of the old nineteenth-century mansion. I could imagine the verbal captions throughout the land: "There, that's it! 'Falcon Crest!' "

The other omission is more difficult to explain. Every time I have pulled into **Christian Brothers**—or considered the turn off North Main Street, St. Helena—tour buses or crowds heading for the auxiliary tasting area have discouraged me. The awesome Greystone Cellars, with its long tasting bar, has been closed while the historic building undergoes repairs to meet earthquake-resistant and structural standards. This huge producer of inexpensive table wines, champagne, and brandy employs about 300 people, the largest in Napa Valley. I have not met Brother Timothy, Christian Brothers' legendary cellarmaster, a blank I would like to fill one day. My objection to **Sterling Vineyards,** between St. Helena and Calistoga, is that it takes an aerial tramway ride to reach its lofty promontory site. I ride tramways only with skis or with small, easily astonished children. But many visitors seem to enjoy the lift to the tasting place.

Beringer   The most visible name and the stately, peaked-roof appearance of the Rhine House attract droves of tourists to this address just north of St. Helena on Route 29. Beringer has been in the wine business since 1867 and stayed with it through the Prohibition period, making medicinal and ceremonial wines and spirits. The Rhine House, now used for offices and as a visitor center, was built in 1883 by Frederick Beringer, who started the winery with his brother Jacob, and the extravagant use the builder made of imported German oak, Pennsylvania slate and Napa Valley cut stone warrants landmark status today. The volume and variety of Beringer wines might be measured by the number of its vineyards, at about a dozen locations from Big Ranch Road near Napa to Knights Valley about 15 miles north of the winery. Beringer's historic presence in California winemaking is also evident in the caves, 1,000 feet in length, which were built late in the nineteenth century and were closed because of earthquake damage in 1906. They have been rehabilitated to store Beringer's Cabernet Sauvignons. Al-

They call it the Rhine House and it was built in the late 1800s by the Beringer brothers after they planted Napa Valley vineyards.

though it is not always easy to edge out of the crowded Beringer parking lot and onto 29 northbound, there is, finally, the reward of driving through a magnificent avenue of shade-giving elms just above the Rhine House. (Phone: 707–963–7115.)

Freemark Abbey   It is sometimes difficult to view this winery from the road (St. Helena Highway North) for the busy tourist complex that now rises before it—the Abbey restaurant, a gourmet shop, a deli, a candle factory, a gift shop. The commercial space is leased by the winery, which has built a strong reputation for consistent, high-on-the-list Cabernets and Chardonnays. The first grapes were planted in the 1870s by a sea captain who acquired the land from California wine pioneer Charles Krug. The original winery was built in the 1880s by a woman, Josephine Tychson, the wife of a Danish immigrant who became ill after buying the property. The following owner, Anton Forni, came up with the enterprising idea of shipping his wine east to the highly concentrated population of Italians who had settled in Barre, Vermont, to work the granite quarries. Neither the red wine market nor the life of the average quarry laborer in northern Vermont lasted very long.

The rejuvenation of Freemark Abbey and its ascent to critical success began with the establishment of a partnership of owners in the late 1960s. If you are not distracted by the restaurant or shops, make it a point to visit the aged stone winery building, attractively sketched on the Freemark Abbey label. (Phone: 707-963-9694.)

Schramsberg Vineyards Near Larkmead Lane, which crosses from 29 to the Silverado Trail just below Calistoga, the winery of Jacob Schram, which impressed author Robert Louis Stevenson (see p. 31) has evolved into a source of delight for connoisseurs of fine sparkling wines. Schramsberg, under the supervision of Jack Davies and his wife Jamie, offers a rewarding chance to touch a historic base before leaving Napa Valley at its northern end. The wine caves dug by Chinese laborers in the 1860s as a practical, low-maintenance way of storing wine have recently been tunneled even deeper into the hillside. Schramsberg is proving that new wine ages very well the old way. (Phone: 707-942-4558.)

SONOMA COUNTY

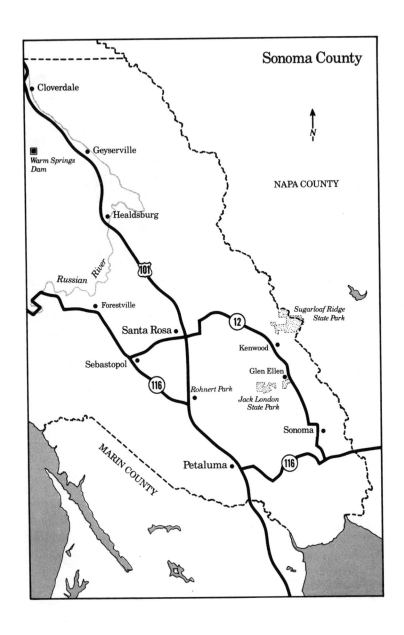

Sonoma

THE small city of Sonoma, at the base of the Sonoma Valley, confronts you with its historic significance on the approach to its wide plaza. Near the end of Broadway—Route 12 direction— the wall of a two-story building is covered by a mural, "Sonoma in the Valley of the Moon," which was sponsored by the Sonoma Valley Historical Society. Even a quick study of the map's features is enough to suggest how much of California history was made within the range of several blocks: the site of the Mission San Francisco Solano (1823); General Mariano Guadalupe Vallejo's first home, La Casa Grande, and the large estate he later occupied, Lachryma Montis; the Sonoma Barracks; the birthplace of the California Bear Flag, which accompanied the capture by American gringos of the Mexican Pueblo of Sonoma in June 1846; the establishment at nearby Buena Vista of the first large experimental vineyards—the budding of the California wine industry—by Hungarian Count Agoston Haraszthy.

The central plaza itself, where Broadway joins East and West Napa Streets, is of historic proportions. It is the largest such civic square in the state, and it reflects the grand scale of General Vallejo's plans when he helped conduct a survey of the land in 1834. A stone city hall now dominates the plaza center, surrounded by shade trees, crosswalks and the bronze figure of a man holding in triumph the Bear Flag of the California Republic. The plaza was dedicated as a National Historic Landmark in 1961. Few American cities can boast of a square of such attractiveness and size (large enough for a civic parade or commemorative fiesta). It is surrounded by many original buildings of Sonoma's past and others that stand on the marked site of Sonoma's early Mexican-American sharing.

I found it helpful in my attempt to sort out local history to begin with Sonoma's beginnings—a visit to **Mission San Francisco Solano** on the corner of First Street East and Spain Street just off the plaza. The site was consecrated in 1823, and the first rough building of what was to become the northernmost of California's 21 missions was completed two years later. Restoration and additions have been made by the state since it acquired the property in the early 1900s; later, it was designated as Sonoma Mission State Historical Monument, a unit of the park system.

The need for a northern mission was felt strongly by Republic of Mexico Governor Luis Arguello, who was concerned about the expansionist tendencies of the Russian fur traders along California's north coast. The governor encouraged Father Jose Altimira to move the established missions at San Francisco and San Raphael in a northerly direction. The young padre was eager and ambitious enough to set out on his own to select a site even before he received approval from superiors in the California missions. Altimira chose well—a place to grow crops, plant orchards, raise livestock—and he named San Francisco Solano for the saint known as the Apostle to the Indies. Church opposition to the padre's independent mission building was finally reduced, and an adobe wing made with sun-dried bricks was added to the original wooden and whitewashed mud building. Now, in its reconstructed shape, it stands as the oldest building in Sonoma.

The mission, like others, was designed for a padre, soldier guards and Indian converts. It was expected to evolve eventually into a parish church. The Indians received religious instruction and were required to help in the fields and with the production of domestic goods. There were nearly 1,000 Indians attached to the mission in 1832. Two years later, the Mexicans disbanded the mission system of extending their frontier and in the following secularization General Vallejo established a pueblo at Sonoma. The town was born; a plaza was laid out.

The site of the last of twenty-one California missions, San Francisco Solano, consecrated in 1823, is preserved near the plaza in Sonoma.

The small adobe church, built at General Vallejo's behest, now appears as a gaudy chapel with piped-in music, which, for me, fails to achieve any ecclesiastical tone. But if the Spanish-mission look is somewhat jarring, I recommend a slow tour in the museum wing, which holds the Virgil Jorgensen Memorial Collection of California Mission paintings. There are 62 original watercolors, the result of a trip taken by artist Chris Jorgensen in 1903–1904, and they leave me with the urge to see all the examples of the Franciscans' impressive heritage.

Solano's courtyard, an area once busy with commerce and the flow of Indians through the mission, has a small garden that invites close study of the common manzanita, the wild strawberry, the poppy, fuschia, Sonoma sage and western columbine. Against the back adobe wall is the stunningly large nopal cactus. The mission is open to the public, 10:00 A.M. to 5:00 P.M. daily; a 50¢ ticket also provides same-day admission to General Vallejo's home, the Sonoma Barracks and the adobe in Petaluma, which Vallejo built for his rancho headquarters—all part of California's Department of Parks and Recreation. For information, call 707–996–1033.

The **Sonoma Barracks**, across First East Street, symbolize the Mexican military hold on the Frontera del Norte when General, Vallejo and his soldiers, supported by the chief of the friendly Suisine tribe (the Indian leader's given Christian name was Francisco Solano), were successfully carrying out raids to eliminate the threat from hostile Indians in the Sonoma vicinity. Commander Vallejo's presidio, begun in the late 1830s, was apparently finished by 1841.

But visitors who tour the barracks, with their displays of frontier weapons, saddles and saddle bags, Indian artifacts, old kilns, freight wagons and a live—and loud—rooster in the courtyard, are drawn by the Bear Flag of the California Republic. It, along with later California flags, is shown on the second floor of the barracks, which is fronted by a wooden balcony overlooking the plaza. The original flag was made of unbleached cloth with a star on one side and a barely recognizable bear opposite; a strip of red flannel was sewn to the bottom of the banner. The star suggested the Lone Star Republic of Texas; the bear apparently was meant to declare the resolute stand of the fledgling republic. But its pudgy shape led some in the Sonoma pueblo to joke that it was more pig than bear.

The crude flag was hurriedly made to signify the victorious "invasion" of the Barracks on June 14, 1846, by three dozen American frontiersmen, resentful of Mexican provincial control and determined to make California as American as Massachusetts. They had been provoked in their revolt—but not personally led—by Captain John C. Frémont, whose party of explorer-adventurers were then in the Sacramento area. The raiders quickly seized supplies, guns, amunition and prisoners, including Vallejo and his military subordinates, who had not resisted. With the success of the Bear Flaggers, Frémont seized Sutter's Fort in the name of the United States and ordered that Vallejo be imprisoned there. The aggressive, independent forays by Frémont and the revolutionaries who rode into Sonoma were made somewhat unnecessary by the fact that the United States had declared war on Mexico. Only a short time later, on June 9, the flag of the California Republic was replaced by the American Stars and Stripes on the pole in Sonoma's plaza.

Vallejo's imprisonment lasted until August, when he was released through the efforts of the American consul in Monterey, Thomas Larkin. There was irony in the "capture" of the Mexican commander by Frémont's adventurers. Vallejo had ordered his presidio detachment to put down arms to avoid bloodshed, believing that the California he knew would inevitably develop under control of Americans who, in increasing numbers, were bringing their skills and ambitions into the territory. Vallejo came back from humiliation at Sutter's Fort to find Sonoma a secure U.S. military garrison and his Petaluma rancho liberated of all livestock and grain supplies by Frémont for his own military use.

Vallejo's encounter with leaders of the Bear Flag group on June 14 took place at La Casa Grande, adjacent to the Barracks. At his home that morning were his brother and military deputy, Salvadore, who lived next door, and his son-in-law, Jacob Leese, whose residence was on the west side of the plaza. The Vallejo home, which sheltered a rapidly expanding family, was the social center of the Sonoma pueblo. It was also the predominant building after the general added a three-story tower at one end of the main house, providing a view of the land far beyond the plaza. The central adobe residence was lost to fire in 1867 but the servants' wing, extending to the rear, still stands. Salvadore Vallejo's house is now the Swiss Hotel, fronting on Spain

General Mariano Vallejo's impressive Petaluma Adobe stands in its modified shape as one of the state's most rewarding historic parks.

Street. Jacob Leese's house, which later quartered U.S. Army officers, remains at the southwest edge of the plaza.

Perhaps it is because there are so many traces of Vallejo preserved from when Alta California was becoming American California that I find it easy to build admiration for the man. As the commandant in Mexico's northern province, he acquired vast landholdings and military power, but when the inevitable change came, stripping him of prestige and wealth, he was progressive enough to adapt and to serve the new landlords as a state senator and as mayor of Sonoma, intelligently bridging the old and new. Following his death at the age of 82, Vallejo was called "the noblest Californian of them all."

I thought of that description one day as I walked the half mile from the plaza to **Lachryma Montis,** which was Vallejo's home for the last 35 years of his life. Part of Sonoma State Historic Park, it can be reached by driving west on Spain Street or by foot on the bicycle and walking path that cuts behind the town parking area near the Barracks. I recommend the easy walk.

Mariano Guadalupe Vallejo was born (1808) and schooled in Monterey. It was his eagerness for education that made him an unusual cadet, later a commissioned ensign, and, in 1830, a member of the legislature. A year later, he was Commander of the Presidio in San Francisco. Vallejo's military and political responsibilities were extended by Governor Jose Figueroa. Vallejo went north along the coast to visit the Russian outpost at Fort Ross—an amicable meeting—and he produced land grants for white settlers in Bodega Bay as part of Mexico's effort to discourage further Russian expansion southward. In the Sonoma and Petaluma valleys, he worked to enlist the support of those Indians willing to stand against tribes hostile to the Spanish presence.

In addition to the small presidio at Sonoma, Vallejo established his own adobe headquarters in the early 1830s on a high rise of land in nearby Petaluma, where, with the help of Indian workers, he would develop his 66,000-acre rancho. (See pp. 80–84 for a description of the largest privately owned adobe building in California, now a historic state park.) Vallejo's Suscol Rancho, above San Pablo Bay, covered 80,000 acres. By the time of the American takeover in the mid-1840s, his land grants totaled approximately 175,000 acres.

Following his election to the new California state senate in 1850, Vallejo made an offer of 150 acres and a large gift of money to build a state capital near the Napa River estuary at the northern end of San Pablo Bay. But plans and the project dragged on while the legislators moved from one site to another before the permanent choice of Sacramento was made. Vallejo did get a town on the bay named for him, although he had proposed to call it Eureka. And when he deeded a piece of Rancho Suscol to Thomas Larkin, the U.S. Consul to Monterey who had eased his prison release at Sutter's Fort, and to Robert Semple, the editor of the *Californian*, a town was named for his wife, Benicia.

But for all of his adobe and town building, General Vallejo settled himself and his family into a relatively modest home. In 1852, he built on a site close to a pool and mountain spring a two-story, wood-frame house he called **Lachryma Montis** (Mountain Tear in Latin). As I approached it along the drive that the general had lined with cottonwood trees and Castilian roses, I was reminded of all the white-fenced, fretworked, gabled houses you see in New England, peaceful and inviting behind their long lawns in the late afternoon. Much of the structure was prefabricated and shipped from the East Coast around Cape Horn. Bricks were added between the walls for insulation against the valley heat of summer, and marble fireplaces were installed in the rooms for winter warmth.

Choose a visiting time well, as I did, and you can tour the 10-room house and hear little but the ticking of the clocks. The atmosphere helps to construct a portrait of Vallejo in the latter part of his life: a rumpled, old-squire's face made round by muttonchop whiskers; the straw hat somehow ill-fitting the man who once rode the frontier with the highest military rank in Alta California. Vallejo's study—the desk, an open diction-ery, a decanter and wine glass, spittoon on the floor—reminds that he was a learned man always eager for more learning. It was said that his library included more than 10,000 books, some of which must have helped him as he wrote his five-volume history of California. (He donated it to the Bancroft Research Library at Berkeley.)

Vallejo's belief in books, in education, was declared early in life when he and his nephew, Juan Batista Alvarado, who be-came the civil leader of the Mexican province at age twenty-seven, were both excommunicated by the Franciscan mission hierarchy for studying the writings of Jean-Jacques Rousseau. Years later, Vallejo sent his son, Platon, east for university training; and his graduation from the Columbia College of Med-icine marked the first time an MD had been given to a Spanish-born student from California. At the outbreak of the Civil War, Vallejo was pleased to assure President Lincoln of the loyalty to the Union of the Spanish Californians.

In an upstairs bedroom of his last *Casa Grande,* I looked through the cathedral-shaped window at the vineyard below and wondered what it must have been like for the old general as he considered his involvement in history, a unique role of militarist turned prominent diplomat. Perhaps, as he ap-proached his death in 1890, he may have taken most pride in his late accomplishments as a horticulturist and a member of the California Horticultural Society. The grounds of his estate at the edge of Sonoma—arbor, gardens, ornate fountains and all —are planted and well maintained for our pleasure today.

I walked back to the town plaza, where despite the historic markers and restored buildings, it is difficult to hold on to an image of Vallejo while passing shops called Total Look, The Sonoma Cheese Factory or Silk & Indigo. On a plaza bench, an elderly man put down his copy of the weekly *Sonoma Index-*

Tribune long enough to give me his capsule description of the town in the mid-1980s. "There's no industry here," he said. "There are few commuters—San Francisco is almost 50 miles away, and you have to go over to Petaluma to catch the bus. We've got vineyards and some big dairy farms. Demands on housing are high because there are a lot of retired people coming in. I read that the median age within the city limits is about 50. You can't tell how much they're worth by the way people dress." He paused and looked up at the sunlight filtered by the thick green foliage. "What it is, is a good place to live."

It was time to consider Sonoma present and past over a Mexican beer at **La Casa**, across the street from Mission San Francisco Solano. It is the town's best and most active Mexican restaurant, with heavy Spanish tables and chairs, tile floors, thick adobe walls and a small bar that serves an astonishing number of icy margaritas at cocktail time, which is almost any time. The guacamole dip and spicy corn chips encourage beer drinking, the tacos and enchilada dishes are zesty, the dark-haired waitresses attractive and nearly always busy. At La Casa, I was encouraged to visit the nearby Depot Museum, sponsored by the Sonoma Valley Historical Society. The hours are somewhat limited: 1:00 to 4:30 P.M., Wednesday through Sunday.

The **Depot Museum** is located behind the public parking area, with its entrance on First Street East; a short walking path leads to the building. The original depot was built in 1880 across the street from the present Swiss Hotel on the plaza. It included a carbarn, a turntable and a coal yard. Railroad parts and castoff materials ended up in the plaza, which "was a weed-filled eyesore" in 1884 according to a local historian. The San Francisco-bound Sonoma Valley Railroad train left the station at 6:10 A.M. and arrived, via a connecting boat, at 9 A.M. Agricultural products were sometimes shipped by rail and then from Schellville, south of Sonoma, by steamboat down Sonoma Creek to San Pablo Bay.

The station was moved in 1890 to its present site, "to accommodate the growing needs of the valley." Until well after World War I, the trains met those needs until local merchants and growers began to depend upon the car and truck. When the depot burned down in 1976, it had been closed for many years.

The replica of the old wooden depot has the stationmaster's office, complete with ticket counter, schedules, brakeman's lantern and other railroad artifacts of a bygone transportation age. The main section of the Depot Museum is devoted to exhibits that relate to the town's past from the 1880s into the 1920s. Millinery displays reveal the contemporary fashions offered at the G. H. Hotz Dry Goods Store, circa 1890. One of the most prominent retail outlets on the plaza, it occupied the building where Simmons Drugs, a vintage apothecary, now does business. Models of a one-room school and of a 1920s kitchen, with the standard Occidental stove, are evidence that growing up in Sonoma was much the same as in any small American town, east or west, 60-odd years ago. The local wine industry that had begun with such early enthusiasm had gone through its first major crisis in the 1870s when the vine pest phyllorexa ruined many vineyards. (Admission to the Depot Museum is 50¢ for adults, 25¢ for youths and senior citizens. Phone: 707–996–1033.)

It was and is an easy walk from the Sonoma station to the **Depot Hotel**, known as the Depot Saloon in the years before Prohibition. In 1890, the owners of this fine-looking, two-story building turned their living room into a bar, the better to greet passengers arriving on the train from San Francisco. Later, they added a dining room. The building went through several owners and uses before, in the mid-1970s, it again became a restaurant with a reputation that has extended well beyond the Sonoma city limits. The new owner-designer created a small bar and dining area on the first floor that leads to a glass-enclosed garden room facing west. Dinner entrees (prix fixe $18) are limited in number but along with the rest of the menu imaginatively prepared. The atmosphere is definitely "a quiet dinner for two." The Depot Hotel is open daily for lunch and for dinner,

5:00 to 9:00 P.M. Sunday brunch 10:30 A.M. to 2:00 P.M. Dinner reservations requested; call 707–938–2980.

A contrasting restaurant setting can be found at **Sharl's**, 136 West Napa Street, where the dining room is spacious, the tables well separated. The French cuisine features the chef's special interest in sauces. For lunch or dinner reservations, call 707–996–5155. **Capri**, 101 East Napa Street, has a familiar-looking French country menu that depends upon fresh produce. The wine list is strong. For reservations, call 707–996–3886. **Gino's** on the plaza at First Street East is popular with lunch crowds and seekers of a Tequila Sunrise, frozen cappuccino, or Tia Maria and coffee. **Pasta Nostra**, 139 East Napa Street, emphasizes hearty veal and spaghetti dishes and says, "The entire menu is available to go."

The Kaboodle is not a restaurant, but this shop just off the plaza is worth a visit if only to admire the most elegantly sweatered teddy bears north of San Francisco.

The list of bed & breakfast possibilities, from Sonoma to Glen Ellen, grows with each season. Advice on accommodations can be obtained by writing or visiting the Sonoma Valley Chamber of Commerce, 453 First Street East on the plaza, Sonoma, 95476 (Phone: 707–996–1033). There is only one motel within the city limits, **El Pueblo**, 896 West Napa Street. Conventional and moderate in price, it is eight blocks west of the plaza. The **Vineyard View**, south of the city at the meeting of routes 116 (Arnold Drive) and 121, is a good choice of economy over luxury. The grouping of stucco, orange-tile-roofed cottages dates back to the 1930s. The units are small and clean, rates under $30. Traffic, aiming for Sonoma, Petaluma or San Francisco rolls by constantly and some of it is diverted to the roadside restaurant across from the motel (early open, early close). Just south on Highway 121 near the airport is the well-supplied Fruit Basket open market. A huge California Co-op Creamery occupies dairylands to the west. It is not easy to view a vineyard from the old motel, but at the overnight rate it doesn't matter.

In Sonoma, the recently expanded **El Dorado Inn** occupies the space of a home built by Salvadore Vallejo. On the northwest corner of the plaza, it is constructed of redwood planking in the popular Monterey Colonial style. The 30 rooms are partially furnished with antiques; rates range from $45 to $70. For reservations call, 707–996–3030. On the opposite corner, at 110 West Spain Street, the smaller **Sonoma Hotel** also has antique-furnished rooms; rates starting at $45. There is an attractive new bar off the quiet lobby. Hotel reservations call 707–996–2996.

The **Sonoma Mission Inn**, on Route 12 in nearby Boyes Hot Springs, is a Spanish revival hotel turned into an all-purpose resort: swimming, tennis and a spa with health and beauty services enough to satisfy the most forlorn guest. The Inn has 97 rooms; rates from $115 to $365 for the master suite; all have canopied beds and are decorated in "soothing" earth tones. If you are not in the mood for a hydrotherapy treatment or an exercise class, you can choose a deep chair in the lobby and listen to the melodic tinkling as the desk summons another bellhop. It is a soothing place for a spot of sherry. For reservations, call 707–996–1041 or write for information to the Sonoma Mission Inn, P.O. Box 1, Boyes Hot Springs, 95416.

Northbound on Route 12, a left turn on Boyes Boulevard leads to the **Sonoma National Golf Course**, which fronts on Arnold Drive. Its fine trees and well-kept greens and fairways make it an inviting sight, even if you have never swung a golf club in frustration. I stopped at the clubhouse late one afternoon for a drink and a little sunset watching as gray-white clouds billowed behind the Sonoma Mountains. A Scottish foursome, who had just finished the 18th hole, took seats at the bar. They were on a vacation tour of selected U.S. courses and were very enthusiastic about the Sonoma National. "It is difficult, quite difficult," one of them said to me. "And it is very beautiful." He waved his hand toward the panoramic view provided by the clubhouse windows.

Arnold Drive joins Route 12 outside Glen Ellen (see Jack London State Historic Park, p. 84). Approximately five miles to the north, Adobe Canyon Road leads to one of the most interesting—and most scenic—parks in the region, **Sugarloaf Ridge**, adjacent to hiking trails developed in Mt. Hood Regional Park. This Mt. Hood is considerably less elevated that the highest peak in Oregon, reaching only 2,730 feet. But that is high ground for the ridge line separating Sonoma and Napa counties.

Sugarloaf Ridge has 25 miles of hiking trails, 50 meadowland campsites and one sizable group camp area. There are corrals and a water trough for horses. The park is ideal for walking or more ambitious uphill hiking, particularly in the spring, fall and winter. In summer, daytime temperatures can discourage one from taking the more difficult routes. If you are on a day visit (the fee is $2, sunup until sundown), there is a short, get-acquainted-with-the-ecology trail of about three quarters of a mile that starts by the parking lot and follows Sonoma Creek to the campfire area. If you admire the West Coast live oak, as I do, think of the tree near the beginning of the trail as once the great food source for the early residents along the headwaters of Sonoma Creek, the Wappo Indians. The tribe depended on the acorns for ground meal, which they converted into mash, soups and cakes. The Wappo resisted the Spanish penetration of their homeland, but their severe enemy was white man's diseases, which drastically reduced their numbers by the mid-1800s.

The trail will take you by a marked cherry-plum tree, a set of Oregon oaks at creekside, an Oregon ash and the huge California laurel. In the spring, snowberries decorate the border of the trails. There is a chance along the way to look westward and see Mt. Hood. The eager hiker can follow the signs to the Bald Mountain Trail, a climb that leads to Red Mountain and Bald Mountain, which is one foot below Mt. Hood's elevation. On a day with good visibility, the peak of the trail pays off with a sweeping look at the distant Sierra Nevada, San Francisco Bay to the south, and, in the 25,000 acres of the park below, contrasting meadowlands and thick chaparral. For additional information, write Sugarload Ridge State Park, 2605 Adobe Canyon Road, Kenwood, 95452, or call 707–833–5712.

Petaluma

The high, rolling country west of Sonoma, with its California Co-operative Creamery farms, may remind Ohioans of Ohio as it recalls part of Vermont to this Vermonter. It is, for several miles, a rich, beautiful land. Route 116 was known as Stage Gulch Road, a transportation link that followed Champlin Creek toward the Petaluma River. As 116 veers southwest to the estuary, a right turn on well-marked Adobe Road leads to the restored headquarters of Vallejo's enormous rancho, now **Petaluma Adobe State Historic Park**. It is, by far, the general's most impressive monument in Northern California.

The two-story building, once the largest private adobe structure in the state, covers a high rise of ground that overlooks the city of Petaluma three miles to the west, its wide river valley and the countryside for miles around. The location, which gave rancheros the security they required a century and a half ago, is impressive today—and so, too, is the building, although in its restored shape it is only half its original quadrangular size.

My first self-guided tour of the adobe was made one midmorning in late winter, with Petaluma white-bright in low sunshine and the surrounding ranchland a lush green. At the edge of the empty parking lot, I stopped to watch a half-dozen lambs busily working the grass. They were oblivious to automotive intrusion of their feeding time. Next to the path on the way to the adobe, resident roosters perched gloomily in a tree, ignoring my passing. They would have fitted appropriately into the landscape when the business of the Vallejo hacienda centered on the raising of sheep, cattle and horses. When I arrived at the open courtyard of the U-shaped adobe, I found the park ranger combing a goat while others stood nearby complaining to her or objecting to my appearance with persistent bleats.

The striking impression of the adobe is its size, designed to serve a community of workers: vaqueros who rode after Vallejo's wide-ranging livestock (an estimated 10,000 to 12,000 cattle plus herds of sheep); hundreds of Indian workers, many of whom had become Christians at the Mission San Francisco Solano; farmers who were responsible for the supplies of grain, fruit and vegetables from nearby fields; the adobe industrialists who made clothing and tools and did the tanning for local use and export. The original building was about 200 by 145 feet; begun around 1834, it used much Indian labor under the supervision of Salvadore Vallejo. The three-foot walls were made of adobe brick, and the roof was apparently thatched and then replaced with redwood shingles.

On the ground level were the kitchen and eating areas, the tool and milling room, the wing for the tannery and tallow making. Vallejo's sleeping and living quarters were on the second floor and the foreman of the rancho occupied one wing. The adobe and the hacienda, which eventually covered about 100 square miles, held an estimated 2,000 Mexican and Indian inhabitants.

I walked through one of the large rooms of the adobe with walls of impressive thickness and learned from the park guidance that it was used to store products of the rancho—chilis and the sacks of tallow so highly valued for trade. This reminded me that candle making was vital to the quality of life at that mid-century point—by stepping onto the well-constructed second-floor balcony I could see the symbols of modern America's needs for energy and light. To the south on Adobe Road is the tall, horizon-cutting power grid of the Pacific Gas & Electric Line Construction Department, its lots heavy with spools of cable.

The exhibits at the adobe make the life of the range-riding vaqueros seem both colorful and romantic, although apparently the cattle were sometimes as wild and unruly as the local bear population. There was nothing but hard labor for the tallow-makers or those who harvested crops by hand in the clay fields.

The productive years of the hacienda were brief. By 1850, with

General Vallejo living in Sonoma and helping to form California's first legislature, the adobe was leased. It was considered as a possible location for the University of California in the mid-1850s. Vallejo finally sold the building and a parcel of adjoining land in 1857. After ownership changes, earthquake and fire, it wasn't until 1951 that the property was taken by the state's Department of Parks and Recreation and the long process of restoration begun. The outcome was one of California's most appealing historic monuments.

Leaving the adobe, you can head for Petaluma on the old Casa Grande Road, once the route of oxcarts to and from the Petaluma River. But where deer and elk fed and played are now the suburban housing extensions of a growing city. Petaluma once promoted itself as "The World's Egg Basket," such was the importance of its poultry business and dairy products. You can still buy Petaluma-incubated eggs in town, but most of the shoppers are likely to be local homeowners who commute to the Bay Area each day.

The tidewater slough that was the important transportation conduit in Vallejo's era extends, with a basin cutoff canal, to the downtown area of Petaluma. But like other sloughs that reach San Pablo Bay, it has been narrowed by silt, and the waterway is used more for recreation than for barge traffic.

Follow the Lakeville Highway beyond the city limits and you get close to the tules and winding waterway of the Petaluma as it broadens toward the bay. In Vallejo's domain, the river ran wide and there was a major boat landing for the flat-bottomed freighters that arrived from San Francisco. Lake Tolay was formed by nearby Tolay Creek. Then as now, the tules were alive with waterfowl.

The sign to the right of the highway that reads "**Gilardi's** Restaurant Tavern/A Beer Experience" introduces one of the more unusual stopping places along the Petaluma River. It is sometimes known as the Lakeville Marina or Gilardi's Resort, but it is best known for its eccentric tavern atmosphere and the original menu offerings by owner Phyllis Lahargoue. The restaurant squats on a rise of ground above a boatyard cluttered with old hulls, marine parts and boats for rent. A nautical road sign points to Liverpool, 5,430 miles, in one direction, and to Yap, 5,341 miles, and Papeete, 4,441 miles, in other directions. The restaurant's wall of windows overlooks this scene and the long stretch of water and thick marsh.

Phyllis Lahargoue, a middle-aged woman with emphatic tastes in food and drink and strong opinions about suitable environments, has owned Gilardi's for eight years. Because of the popularity of her live jazz and bluegrass music nights, she has expanded her window view of the world. I sat with her at the comfortable bar-counter that offers daily wine specials and "99 different beers." Actually, she said, she stocked 104 of the world's best, but the number 99 was chosen to harmonize with the words of the old drinking song.

The menu changes each day, and you have to examine the refrigerator door where the specials are written out with a Sanford Expo pen. You may find calamari, snapper Vera Cruz, cabbage rolls and fritatta scrawled above the chili, burgers and a variety of soups. The salads come with a house dressing Phyllis creates with apple cider vinegar, oil and honey. She gets a lot of requests for the recipe and for hints about how she makes her rhubarb and apple pies. If you don't want wine or are bewildered by the choice of brews, you might go for the black currant iced tea.

We watched a blue heron standing straight and still against the line of bulrushes, and it reminded her of a recent early morning when she arrived as a heavy tule fog gradually lifted from the river. "I looked down the edge of the water and saw these white symbols lined up about 25-feet apart all the way down," she said. "I thought, my Lord, they have come overnight and surveyed and put down their stakes. Then, slowly, I could see them—egrets standing equally spaced and so many of them. Amazing! Sometimes early I can see the sun coming up over there and the full moon in the sky there"—and she pointed toward the bank of windows. "I chose this place," she said. "And you might say it chose me to do what I wanted with it and run my kind of a joint."

Gilardi's is at 5688 Lakeville Highway, Petaluma. (Phone: 707–762–4900).

For more conventional dining surroundings and inspired California preparations, the **Opera House Cafe** attracts local and long-range customers to a renovated building in the downtown section of Petaluma not far from the Hill Plaza Park. Open Thursday through Sunday, the Opera House Cafe is at 145 Kentucky Street. For hours and reservations, call 707–765–4402,

Glen Ellen/Jack London State Historic Park

Ahead and toward the right, across sheer ridges of the
  mountains,
separated by deep green canyons and broadening lower down
  into rolling
orchards and vineyards, they caught their first sight of
  Sonoma Valley
and the wild mountains that rimmed its eastern side.
                    —Jack London, *The Valley of the Moon*

If Jack London needed to think himself a superman, as critics have suggested, the status would seem to have been granted him when, many years following his death in 1916, a large state park was established in his honor. Perhaps no other American author's name has been preserved in such grand fashion. **Jack London State Historic Park**, 803 acres, is an uphill mile west of Glen Ellen, in the Valley of the Moon just north of Sonoma. The park includes the ruins of Wolf House, the 26-room home London built but was never able to live in, the modest burial site nearby, part of the 1,400-acre ranch he developed beneath Sonoma Mountain, and the House of Happy Walls, which his

The House of Happy Walls, built by Jack London's widow, is a large stone monument to the author and a museum of collections from London's life.

wife built as a memorial and which now serves as a museum.

One need not even be a one-time reader of Jack London's stories to be impressed with the scope of his interests and the manner in which he chose to live in the years preceding his death at age forty. Many of his triumphs and the symbols of his defeats are on view in the park. It is worth a lengthy visit. I head directly to the rambling fieldstone mansion Charmian London built in 1919, set among redwood, Douglas fir and live oak. It houses the books and biographical artifacts, including the South Sea collection the author gathered on his trip in his famous ketch-rig vessel, the *Snark.* I am drawn to the display of his writings, which begins with a rejection letter from the *Oakland Bulletin,* dated September 17, 1898—the first of some 600 rejection slips he received in his writing career. His 4,000-word story described a journey he took by small boat on the Yukon. But the prolific London—later, internationally acclaimed—traveled a far distance after that turndown, which is shown in a case display of foreign editions of his books, most prominent are *White Fang* and *The Call of the Wild.* There are translations in Bengali, Latvian, Polish, Arabic, Japanese, Hebrew and a volume in Russian.

With the Holman collection of first editions of 48 of his works is the quote: "I am a believer in regular work, and never wait for an inspiration." The reproduction of London's study suggests this functional attitude: a standard folding typewriter with wooden case, a rolltop desk, a Victor gramaphone, a dictating machine and a world globe. I have trouble visualizing one of the world's best-known authors during the early part of the century sitting in the small wooden swivel chair and pounding away at yet another novel or *Saturday Evening Post* story.

London's early identification with the working class, which began in the Bay Area (where he was born in 1876) and his activist role in the labor movement are documented in letters and mementoes. Charmian's membership card in the Socialist Party of America is displayed near Jack's resignation letter of 1916. He faulted the party for its "lack of fire and fight and its loss of emphasis on the class struggle." It is signed "Yours for the revolution."

Before taking the half-mile walk to the ruins of Wolf House, it helps to study the architect's drawing of the floor plans in the museum and to realize that many of the room furnishings and the acquisitions here were supposed to become part of the house that Jack built and was destroyed by fire shortly before the Londons were due to move in. It was a writer's dream house: 26 rooms, nine fireplaces, an interior courtyard with reflection pool, a space designated as "Jack's sleeping tower," a fireproof vault for manuscripts. The final cost was estimated at about $80,000.

The path taken in winter can be a silent walk through tall oaks brightened at the top by slanting sunlight. Approaching the giant stone skeleton of the building can be an eerie experience. "My house will be standing, act of God permitting, for a thousand years," he wrote. Its basic materials strengthened the intention: lava stone, unpeeled redwood logs and Spanish tile. What remains is hardly the Colosseum, yet it is ancient and awesome with towering chimneys and heavy walls braced with steel and darkened with moss. Gone without a trace are Jack's work den and Charmian's apartment. At the second-floor level, rainwater sits in the reflection pool and the diagram at the viewing area makes it possible to visualize the pergola, the library, the music room and Jack's gun-and-trophy room. On a rise behind the ruins, a fine stand of redwoods has grown strong over the years, high enough surely to reach above Jack's sleeping tower.

Sometime before his death (the copy of the death certificate in the museum records the cause as "uraemia following renal colic"), London told Charmian, "I wouldn't mind if you laid my ashes on the knoll where the Greenlaw children [neighbors] are buried. And roll over me a red boulder from the ruins of the home." The gravesite is a short walk on a signed path from the remains of Wolf House. Charmian's ashes were also placed there behind the small wooden picket fence in 1955.

London died in the cottage next to old winery buildings he purchased in 1911 as part of what he called "Beauty Ranch." It is across the access road from the museum and should be the next goal in a park visit. But the cottage, where London wrote his later books and stories, has to be viewed in the context of his ranch and the exceedingly ambitious agrarian experimenting that went on under his direction. "I see my farm in terms of the world and the world in terms of my farm," he wrote. In his scientific-ranching efforts, he planted spineless cactus for cattle feed (then recommended by Luther Burbank), terraced hillsides to check erosion, grew nearly 150,000 eucalyptus trees as rapid-growth hardwoods. This experiment cost him $50,000, and he ended up with more firewood than all the chimneys of Wolf House could ever handle. His Angora herd and his pigs became diseased, even though he maintained the pigs in a uniquely designed round "Pig Palace." It stands as an impressive piggery today. London was proud of his purebred English shire horses, which fitted the image in his boast: "I am the sailor on horseback! Watch my dust! Oh, I shall make mistakes a-many;

but watch my dream come true." London apparently did ride his ranch as an authoritarian sailor on horseback; his regimented support staff grew to more than 40 people.

A tour of the ranch center covers slightly more than a half mile. It passes the old Kohler & Frohling Winery building London used as a stable for his prize horses; another stone horsebarn built in 1914; a huge shell of a winery building, damaged in the earthquake of 1906 and used in part as a carriage house and quarters for ranchhands and guests; and "The Cottage," a low, sprawling frame building with a tall-windowed study facing west and a glassed-in porch where the author died. The east wing of the house was an attached stone winery building that the Londons used as a dining hall. "The Cottage" is not in shape for visitors, but it can be peered into. It is the top priority of a major fund drive to restore the buildings on Beauty Ranch. But even in their decaying state, they fit gracefully into the bowl of land below the mountain. A half-mile-plus trail walk takes you to the five-acre lake London created as a reservoir and used for swimming parties. Both hiking and horseback trails extend up the 2,300-foot summit of Sonoma Mountain. The climb of more than three miles—through madrone and manzanita, oak and redwood—offers the chance to view from rewarding levels the valley London celebrated. London is probably better remembered for his hobo recollections than for his career as a grand-style rancher, but it is our happy advantage that the state of California has chosen to preserve the site of the sailor on horseback's last stand.

Glen Ellen sits in a small way at the foot of the approach to Jack London State Park, on Arnold Drive, which parallels Route 12 from Sonoma. When you have checked out Bill's Glen Ellen Hardware, the Hungry Wolf deli, Bob Marshall's body works, the two groceries and the post office and wondered about the possibilities for the vacant brick hotel bearing the date 1906, you have done much of the town. I have stayed in the standard

and convenient **London Lodge** on the corner and found suitable food and drink at the adjoining Jack London Saloon and
Restaurant. A glass of River Bend Chardonnay at the bar was
$2.25, and the cheaper jug white was Valley of the Moon from
the winery just down the road. The restaurant, with tables
overlooking slow-running Sonoma Creek, offers hearty T-bones,
prime ribs, scaloppine, pasta. The luncheon hamburgers are
first-rate.

A short distance south on Arnold Drive, the **Grist Mill Inn**,
"A tradition for 128 years," presents a modern restaurant in an
old setting behind a winery building. The atmosphere is dark-
wood pleasant, the moderately priced entrees are well prepared
on mesquite charcoal. I was there in the off-season and it was
open for dinner only. Across the road, the *Jack London Book
Store* is stocked with used books, Jack London memorabilia, and
an impressive number of London titles.

Santa Rosa

Travelers may find Santa Rosa too similar to what they left
behind in order to get where they are going: the Sonoma Valley
wine country, the redwoods, the Russian River region, the dramatic northern coastline. Santa Rosa seems to start somewhere
around the planned villages and new corporate headquarters of
Rohnert Park off Highway 101 and stretch north another 17
miles or more to Windsor, where mobile home parks dominate
the landscape. Santa Rosa has grown east along Route 12 to
Oakmont and west to Sebastopol. The city limits do not reach
that far, but the metro sprawl of this county seat—a major
residential-industrial center—does. It epitomizes middle-city
growth.

Horticulturist Luther Burbank had the pleasure of reacting
to the very sprouting of Santa Rosa when he arrived from Massachusetts in 1875. "I firmly believe from what I have seen," he

wrote, "that it is the chosen spot of all this earth as far as nature is concerned, and the people are better than the average."

Burbank exclaimed over the great shade oaks, the 12-foot high fuchsias, the roses climbing over the small houses. The oaks still shade Santa Rosa streets, the roses bloom, but there is little impressive about Luther Burbank Gardens, the small downtown park. In adjoining Juilliard Park, The Church-of-One-Tree, constructed from a single Guerneville redwood, was drawing most attention on the day of my visit. The large Burbank Center for the Arts is worth a turn off 101 just north of the city limits. But famous nursery experimenter Burbank is celebrated seasonally by all the amateur backyard growers of vegetables, fruits and flowers in this favored area.

I asked a Santa Rosa resident for a selective summary of local attractions and her reply was: "Well, we *do* have the large County Fairgrounds, and you can play golf there right in the middle of the racetrack the year around!" But she pointed me toward the old Railroad Square district at Fourth and Wilson Streets, by Santa Rosa Creek, as a model of a downtown restoration that combines old stone architecture, long-serving restaurants and bars, a working vaudeville theatre. She said that even the very new shops in the old warehouse buildings fitted in acceptably.

I was attracted to the depot building itself, a classic western passenger station built of stone from local quarries. If you recall a scene or two from Alfred Hitchcock's *Shadow of a Doubt*, with Teresa Wright and Joseph Cotton, you have seen the railroad station and near blocks through Hitchcock's eyes. For authentic railroad sights and sounds today at the depot you have to be lucky enough to have a Northwestern Pacific freight rumble slowly along the line.

Another landmark, early-century stone building gives Railroad Square distinction: the renovated (at a cost of more than $6 million) Hotel La Rose, named for St. Rose of Lima, which gave the city some fame early in the nineteenth century. It is a worthy civic effort to pull travelers off the nearby high-speed, elevated highway and get them to spend a night down by the depot of this old valley town.

Occidental

Not all roads lead from Santa Rosa, Sebastopol, Bodega and the Russian River to the tiny town of Occidental, but several do, and they are apt to be rolling with traffic headed for a family-style Italian dinner. Occidental is the place where pasta—very generous helpings of it—is a vital link in the local economy. Three large Italian restaurants are located along the five-block main street that parallels the Bohemian Highway.

The **Union Hotel** dates from 1879 when Occidental was on its way to becoming a busy rail terminus. It now includes a spacious restaurant area; a renovated saloon; the Bocce Ballroom, which features live music; and an adjacent motel (convenient for those travelers who have taken to the food and wine too enthusiastically).

The restaurant's long-lasting success is the result of the consistent quality and size of the dinner portions and the moderate prices. A spaghetti dinner with serve-yourself soup and salad runs $5.95; the complete family-style chicken dinner with antipasto is $7.50. My first such performance at the Union Hotel left the waitress dismayed. She appeared swiftly at my table, her serving wagon loaded with Italian bread, a hefty salad, a tureen of minestrone soup. I noticed that her apron matched my tablecloth. Even though I dished out only a half bowl of minestrone, I could make but a small dent in the ravioli. "You should have asked for a children's portion," she admonished. Indeed I was surrounded by large tables of hearty, happy, have-some-more-wine diners whose only cautions were: "Watch the garlic! Watch the garlic!"

Fiori's and **Negri**'s compete with the renowned Union restaurant for the Italian family-style appetites that visitors bring to Occidental. If you somehow can't face up to a one-quart serving of soup or a similar quantity of ravioli at bargain rates, you can follow locals, as I did one midday, to the **Third Street Depot Deli** for a sandwich or a cup of chili and a beer. Outside the town library, where the morning sun had finally cleared the forested hills that are Occidental's backdrop, a man braced with two canes and showing a weathered smile spoke about the Union Hotel and its reputation.

"It's been in the same family since I can remember, and I've lived here many years," he said. "I used to think I was quite a trencherman but they serve more than I can handle now. It *is* good food. You can't beat it. Hell, don't people come to the hotel from hundreds of miles!" He said that Occidental was once a stage stop and later the place where trains to and from Camp Meeker turned around. "The train crews stopped over here and the hotels went up. The first one was the old Summit House."

The Bohemian Highway out of Occidental follows Dutch Bill Creek past Camp Meeker, so dark in the shadows of dense redwoods that it is hard to recognize as a community. The highway leads to Monte Rio (River Mountain), a town on the Russian River and below nonlofty Mt. Heller, less than 1,000 feet. Drive across Moscow Road and the bridge, and Route 116 west, which traces the Russian River's course, will take you to the nearby town of Duncans Mills. A too-new historical recreation, the town developed around a sawmill started by Duncans in 1860. Tourists are encouraged to visit the Depot Museum, where some well-preserved railroading equipment is on display, including a 1902 North Shore Railroad passenger car. Duncans Mills was then linked to Marin County by rail. Standing apart from old Duncans Mills is the **Blue Heron Inn**, whose mixed menu ("International vegetarian specialties," fish, Mexican dishes) and bar are popular with area residents.

Russian River Resorts

It is only a half-dozen miles from Duncans Mills to the mouth of the Russian River and then north to Jenner (see p. 109). In the opposite direction on 116 are many bends in the river and an unbroken chain of camps and resorts that leaves no turn undeveloped for miles.

The Indians called the river the Shabaikai (long snake) and the Russian settlers referred to it as "the charming little one." By any name, the river, after its smooth flow through the Alexander Valley, adopted a tortuous course as it veered west toward the sea. A mile above Monte Rio, the tall redwoods of Bohemian Grove march from the edge of the river to shield an exclusive colony, the members-only Bohemian Club of San Francisco, which has gathered here in summer since the 1870s. A couple of sharp bends upriver, the town of Guerneville (for early mill owner George Guerne) offers the sort of nonexclusive facilities that occupy most banks of the Russian River. Motels, redwood resorts with riparian names, beach areas, a kiddie amusement park, rent-a-trailer signs, posters for a rock-skipping contest, overnight and weekly rate accommodations for families, fishermen and the expanding number of gays who favor the area—all vie for space and attention along the roadway. The confused first-time visitor should take comfort that the adult resorts and campsites are well labeled as such, and the conventional family facilities can be identified by the noise and numbers of children in the swimming pool.

At Guerneville's center, where Route 116 joins eastbound River Road, Armstrong Woods Road points north to an unusually attractive redwoods reserve only three miles out of town. **Armstrong Woods**, a 700-acre state park, is named for nineteenth-century lumberman Colonel James Armstrong who donated land for a park and botanic garden for public enjoyment. The preserve may be small in dimension, but the trees are impressively tall. One of them, the Parson Jones Tree, is about

310 feet. The Armstrong Redwoods, perfect for viewing on an afternoon stroll, are connected to the **Austin Creek State Recreation Area**, 4,200 acres of varied terrain. The parkland has a limited number of campsites and some hiking elevations that approach 1,900 feet. It appeals to riders because the trails are open to horses; parking for horse trailers is available near the entrance of Armstrong Woods.

Because of resort crowding and beach use, the Russian River is, at this extremity, hardly the flowing fishing stream it once was. Yet, even in summer, when the heat is up and the water level down, fishermen are on the banks angling for bass or bluegill or catfish. When the fall rains come and the tourists stay away, the river is more seriously fished by pursuers of the migrating steelhead, the species of rainbow trout that turns a steely blue during its time in the Pacific. In the winter of 1986 rains churned the Russian into a destructive force, causing heavy damage in the Guerneville area.

The steelhead run has been steadily reduced by all the familiar environmental negatives, from casual dumping to the churning of the river bottom by dune buggies. But the fishermen still come with the modest hope of pulling out a 10-pounder. At a sports supply store in Guerneville, a man in waders who had been selecting new leaders said that the run was now best from Rio Nido to Guerneville, about a two-mile stretch. Earlier that morning he had taken a stock steelhead near Rio Nido and then released it. The success of the catch was enough on this wet-cold day. The Russian was running much higher than when I had seen it in early fall, I said. The fisherman smiled, politely enough. "You should see it real angry. If you live down around Duncans Mills—or even here—the river can get as rough as the ocean it's about to meet."

Healdsburg

In the warm, inviting spring of 1985, the city of Healdsburg, 14 miles north of Santa Rosa, was afflicted by a streak of graffiti vandalism one might expect to encounter in a divided resort community along the Mediterranean. "Locals Only" signs and other antivisitor slogans began to appear on buildings. The brief underground campaign distressed city officials anxious to lift tourist trade, but it confirmed an impression I had about Healdsburg. There is an attractiveness about this Alexander Valley community well worth protecting, and not much of it is visible as one drives along Healdsburg Avenue to the Simi Winery, the main tourist target at the north side of town.

Healdsburg is looped by the Russian River, which cuts around Fitch Mountain, the city's redwood backdrop. Spacious Victorian and modern houses and small Adirondacks-style camps perch above the river close to Fitch Mountain Road. An unpretentious golf course wanders up the foot of the hill. Below that is a spacious recreation area that includes a vintage wooden ballpark built in the early 1930s. Healdsburg has a town beach of typically limited Russian River size, with canoe rentals nearby. The city plaza, planted with palms and redwoods and centered around a fountain, was laid out in 1857, and the buildings facing it struggle to meet the proper proportions of commercial and historic. But the city keeps trying.

Healdsburg is favored by its location, as the ranchers and fruit growers of the past and the vineyard owners of the present would indicate. Long before white settlers took advantage of the valley, the Southern Pomo fished and hunted here. By the 1840s, the Mexican government had granted the Indian lands to a sea captain named Henry Delano Fitch. In 1845, Cyrus Alexander, chosen by Fitch to oversee his 48,000-acre rancho, settled northeast of the present city and began to develop one of the major cattle ranches in Northern California. Fitch and Alexander left their imprint and names on the territory, and so did Harmon

G. Heald, an Ohio native who built a trading post on a site near the plaza on Healdsburg Avenue. Since Harmon Heald opened his general store in 1852, the local population has grown to about 7,500.

Healdsburg still has characteristics of an agricultural center, and fruit, grain and grapes grown in the vicinity are important to the economy. The Farmers Market on East and Haydon Streets sells local produce during limited hours from May until early fall. On Dry Creek Road, at the edge of town, Timber Crest Farms offers tours of its organic processing facilities for a variety of nuts and fruits. Healdsburg is the home of wineries, all within easy reach and each with its own physical distinction. They are described on pages 119–120.

Whether by accident or intention, Healdsburg does have an assortment of picnic places: the town plaza, the recreation park at University and Piper Streets, Villa Chanticleer (the city-owned conference center with an adjacent park on North Fitch Mountain Road) and Memorial Beach and Park, which are just across the Russian River Bridge. The wineries, most notably Simi, have outdoor table areas for visitors. I found a couple of ideal alfresco spots along the Northwestern Pacific Railroad tracks that best remain undesignated.

A light picnic or a hearty breakfast at the tiny and locally popular **Singletree**, located at 217 Healdsburg Avenue near the Chamber of Commerce, is a pleasant way to lead up to an exceptional dining experience at **Madrona Manor**. The highly recommended restaurant is a short distance beyond the city limits on Westside Road, which tracks the Russian River valley. Built in 1881 as a summer home by a wealthy San Franciscan, this old rural residence too grand for practical use today stands at the top of a gravel-dirt road. But the three-story Victorian mansion and surrounding buildings have been developed into an unusual bed & breakfast inn. The appeal of dining at Madrona Manor comes not only from the elegant surroundings, but also from the work of the staff in and out of the high-ceilinged dining rooms and, of course, the kitchen and the chefs' creative use of the mesquite grill, the bread oven and the smokehouse. A table set with fresh flowers looks out on a balcony where you can imagine the proper young women in long lavender dresses waving their greeting to house guests arriving on the carriage road below. But it takes no imagination to enjoy the smoked chicken salad with Belgian endive, walnuts and apples or an entree of roasted quail stuffed with wild mushrooms. The Manor's wine list includes imports and modestly priced bottles from nearby vineyards. Dinner menus are a la carte Sunday through Thursday and prix fixe Friday and Saturday. There is a Sunday brunch, 10:30A.M. to 2:30 P.M. Breakfast is served to guests only. B & B room rates are $80 to $125. For reservations and dinner information, call 707–433–4231.

Among the motels in or close to Healdsburg, the **L & M**, at 70 Healdsburg Avenue, is moderate and well maintained (Phone: 707–433–6528). On the town plaza, the small **Healdsburg Inn** provides a renovated Victorian interior (Phone: 707–433–6991). On Dry Creek Road, the **Dry Creek Inn**, operated by Best Western, looms institutionally large by Highway 101 (Phone: 707–433–0300).

Geyserville and Cloverdale

The first time I was in Geyserville I walked beyond empty vineyards and went swimming in the Russian River. The experience, on one of those fall days of the postharvest heat, which quickly builds in the Alexander Valley, left me with a very buoyant feeling about Geyserville that hasn't been reduced by several visits since. A good part of the town's charm is that it doesn't strive for any. A large mural on a building wall in what passes for the commercial center depicts Geyserville's lively "legend of yesteryear." The first house had a lifespan from 1851, when Geyserville was established, until 1930. The third and last train depot was demolished in 1970 after nearly 100 years of train service. The Depot Hotel went down in flames in 1933 but the Geyserville Hotel stood from 1876 until 1940. Geyserville serves its 1980s visitors and a population of about 1,000 with a limited number of unpretentious businesses on its main street.

The town's community leaders have been trying to adopt development guidelines that will preserve the friendly atmosphere and prohibit the touristy gaudiness and instant restoration that characterize nearby localities. Geyserville is closely connected to heavily traveled tourist paths. Four name wineries —Geyser Peak, Pedroncelli, Souverain, Pastori—are nearby. The Lake Sonoma recreation area is just west of town, and Canyon Road, which joins Geyserville Avenue, is a main exit on 101 to the lake. Farther east are geothermal steam fields that culminate beyond Sulphur Peak at The Geysers.

In keeping with its slow-to-change attitude, Geyserville has one main eating-and-drinking establishment, which has been in business since 1936. **Catelli's the Rex** is a family-owned Italian restaurant in the business block on Geyserville Avenue. Menu and bar prices are moderate, tables for lunch and dinner are busy, and reservations are requested for groups of five or more. (Phone: 707–857–9904.) One lunch hour at Catelli's I encountered a group of local people reviewing plans for the annual blood bank drive, held at the old clapboard Grange Hall just across the Russian River on Route 128. "For a pint of blood," I was told, "you get to come to the free barbecue—all the beef or wild pig or clams you want to eat. Free wine and beer, too. We've got over eleven hundred pints in the bank, and this town's population is a little less than that." I had to decline, but I did visit the Grange Hall where the blood-drawing was scheduled a few days later in early April.

Souverain Cellars, the elaborately designed winery with twin hop kiln towers on Independence Lane south of Geyserville, has a large restaurant facility open for lunch and dinner.

The winery is also the site of concerts, plays and grape-stomp festivals during the year. For reservations and information, call 707-433-8281. (For comment on Geyser Peak, Pedroncelli and Pastori wineries, see pages 122-125.)

Warm Springs Dam and Lake Sonoma—take Canyon Road to Dry Creek Road—is a massive Army Corps of Engineers' project that offers public picnic grounds, a steelhead fish hatchery and a visitor center with exhibit areas. The 319-foot-high earth-fill dam, erected for flood protection and water supply, has provided a flood-pool-lake-area of 3,600 areas—a vast stretch of Dry Creek blue as seen from the overlook area. A tour of the hatchery, a picnic and a lake visit can be easily fitted into a half-day trip.

Cloverdale lies less than 10 miles north of Lake Sonoma—Route 101 runs through the center of this small city of 4,500. There are more than two dozen small manufacturing plants in the community area, but citrus long ago provided the town with its major distinction. The annual Fruit Festival in February attracts visitors from throughout Northern California. At **Zola's Restaurant**, whose dining room has louvered picture windows looking out on the passing automotive parade on 101, I asked why Cloverdale was so slow in removing its civic Christmas decorations. "Oh, they stay up until the Fruit Festival!" was the logical answer.

SONOMA COAST

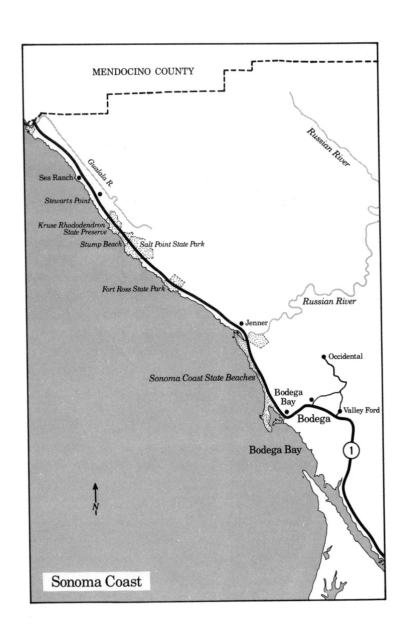

MENDOCINO COUNTY

Russian River

Sea Ranch

Gualala R.

Stewarts Point

Kruse Rhododendron
State Preserve

Stump Beach   Salt Point State Park

Fort Ross State Park

Russian River

Jenner

Occidental

Sonoma Coast State Beaches

Bodega
Bay

Valley Ford

Bodega

Bodega Bay

①

N

Sonoma Coast

Bodega Bay

A MONG the several approaches to Bodega Bay—by sea, coastal highway, overland—I choose by habit the Bodega Highway out of Sebastopol, past those prosperous California Co-op Creamery farms with their Dairy Merit Award signs, past the lengthy white fences of St. Anthony's Farm, which supplies its San Francisco mission. If you take the branch to Valley Ford, you can reach an exalted mood for the approaching seascape as you drive through sweeps of green pastureland. Valley Ford, more old than new, was a dairy town with a name acquired from an Indian trail—a valley ford—that crossed the head of the Estero de Americano, a tidal creek that now marks the Sonoma-Marin county boundaries. Highway 1 from Valley Ford encourages me to take the short spur to the town of Bodega, which sits just over the coastal hills from the harbor.

Bodega—resting place in Spanish—has a historic schoolhouse, a white-steepled church, and clusters of sheep on uphill meadows. St. Teresa's, built in 1861 and selected as a historical landmark in 1967, is the oldest Catholic church in the county. The Watson District School was opened in 1856 and the schoolhouse and its belltower are preserved in a small, county-maintained wayside park. The school is named for a wealthy potato farmer, James Watson, who made his fortune growing Bodega reds. Nearby, the former Potter School, built in 1873 on land donated by Sheriff Potter, houses a restaurant and gallery. When I last visited the gallery, paintings by regionalists from the Tomales Bay area were on display.

Bodega Bay bears the name of its discoverer, Juan Francisco de la Bodega y Cuadra, who was exploring the area by schooner in 1775. He was followed by Russians who sailed down the coast from Alaska and found that they could grow grain on land and make their haul of sea otter skins, too. It wasn't until the late 1840s that Captain Stephen Smith, with a Mexican land grant, opened a warehouse that provided the start for a port town. Bodega Bay's proximity to San Francisco enabled it to develop quickly as a freight and passenger center on the coast. But it gradually fell victim to shifting sand, and the well-protected harbor, with high headland toward the ocean and long sandspit from the mainland, became virtually useless for ships of size. *The WPA Guide to California,* describing the port in the late 1930s, commented: "Bodega Bay is now a shallow, sand-choked inlet, rimmed by mud flats at low tide; its egress to the sea on the south side is blocked. . . . Vessels no longer call here—nor have they for a generation past."

All that has been changed by dredging and marine maintenance plus the demands of sports and commercial fishing interests. The sandspit, now **Doran County Park**, arches toward the bay and Bodega Rock and has been groomed for a launching ramp, more than 130 camping spaces and picnic tables for day use. The U.S. Coast Guard station looks out at the well-marked —and often busy—channel.

On a late January day, I paid the $2 nonresident fee and drove along Doran Beach Road with an excess of parking choices. There was a single camper, with an elderly couple reading underneath their canopy. But I soon attracted an audience of large gulls, who roosted on picnic tables, the chained trash cans and posts or hunched in sun-bright parking spaces. I brooded about *The Birds,* Hitchcock's famous movie that was filmed in the area—and questioned my picnic decision. I quick-counted 24 seabirds watching me: California gulls, darker western gulls, maybe a ring-tailed gull. At the Sonoma County Park bulletin board, I read that the Farallon Islands to the south constitute one of the largest seabird nesting areas in the country. Murres, petrels, puffins and gulls breed there, but here I was definitely in all-gull company. Not a leftover blue heron or white egret in sight, no double-breasted cormorant or western grebe, supposedly common to these harbor waters. The crabbing guide on the board reminded of the need for a measuring device and listed the various limits: for the popular Dungeness, the limit is 10, minimum size is 6¼ inches. The crab season runs from the second Tuesday in November until June 30. The information continued: "27 species of marine mammals utilize the area, including a variety of whales, dolphins, porpoises, harbor seals and sea lions." But one has to go across the harbor to the state beach and Bodega Head for such sightings. I decided to eat my smoked salmon sandwich and ignore the glowering, Hitchcock-size gulls. The low January sun, the occasional channel passing of a fishing boat, the strong light on the tiled roofs of Bodega Bay's hillside community, comprised a scene of midwinter beauty.

My first of periodic failures at whale watching (see pp. 161–163 for greater whale detail) came in this winter season at Bodega Head, reached by the Bay Flat Road and the continuing West Side Road, off Highway 1 at the north edge of the harbor. I prefer to start at Doran Beach and then go to the wilder ocean side, with its great bluffs thrusting out toward the rising and falling sea. The road leads to Masons Marina, with its berths, hoists, docks—and often a dredger at work. The Sonoma County Regional Parks Department is developing a marina at nearby Spud Point, with the commercial fisherman—and not the potato shipper—in mind. About 80% of the 250-berth facility is designed for commercial use, the rest for recreational boats. The entrance to the University of California Biological Research Lab is on the West Side Road. The center, where studies in aquaculture and marine pollution are conducted, is open to the public on most Friday afternoons.

At Bodega Head, I found a few whale watchers, their telescopic-lensed cameras on tripods and binoculars at the ready, waiting for evidence in the great expanse of bobbing sea of the southbound migrating California grays. But they soon gave up staring at the hypnotic Pacific, packed their gear and left. I walked a couple of trails that cross the headland park and considered both the beauty of the ocean from these heights and the dangers, the daily challenge, it meant for the fishermen who depart from the safety of Bodega Bay each day.

Between the spring of 1984 and early 1985, eight fishermen were lost, an unprecedented number for this small town. Some blamed tougher fishing restrictions and the cost of equipment that pushed men to take their boats out farther, no matter how foul the weather, in order to make each fishing day count. Victims included steel-hulled drag boats capable of hauling 30,000 pounds of fish and smaller single-handed vessels that were suddenly capsized by a rogue wave. Bodega Bay holds an annual Fisherman's Festival in the spring, with a traditional blessing of the fleet. The 1985 celebration involved many local people who in the previous year had mourned the loss of a friend or relative at sea.

At the Tides Wharf—sport fishing rentals, daily charter boat sailings, and commercial moorings—I talked to a fisherman who was priming his generator as he prepared for a crab run. He goes out every day the weather allows. He said he grew up in Bodega Bay, moved to Eureka but was discouraged by the restrictions on commercial salmon fishing in the north. "This is still a fishing town," he said. "But you look at all the expensive houses"—and he gestured toward the Bodega Harbour Development—"and you wonder."

Other fishermen say they can no longer afford to live in the area or eat in restaurants priced for the tourist trade, so they sleep on their boats during the crab season. The expanded Tides Inn, the recently finished Lucas Wharf restaurant, the arrival of boutiques at the Pelican Plaza shopping center, all signal the Bay Area's changed role. The fishing town's main catch is tourists and new investors.

·   ·   ·

The admirably placed **Bodega Bay Lodge** stretches above the south end of the harbor and is fronted by sea grass and favored with a view of Doran Beach, the bay with its guardian Bodega Rock and, of course, the harbor. I recommend it for its rooms with wide, western-facing windows and private balconies, the wicker furnishings and useful kitchenette facilities. A glass-walled whirlpool spa and swimming pool is landscaped on the harbor side of the lodge. The Bodega Bay golf course is next door. (Double rooms with kitchenette are $72 in the off-season; with fireplace, $84. Continental breakfast included.) For reservations, call 707-875-3525 or call Best Western Reservations Center.

The Tides Wharf is your all-purpose, nautical visitor center: busy seafood restaurant and bar, beer and liquor outlet, fish wholesale and retail. Plus the commercial activity of the wharf —fishermen maintaining their boats, bright orange fishing nets drying in the sun—all that camera buffs could ask for in local color. The Tides Motel is opposite the wharf on Highway 1.

Lucas Wharf Restaurant and Bar is a new, large-capacity sea grotto, with a quick approach off Highway 1. Lucas Wharf's takeout seafood sandwiches are ideal for a park lunch. **The Whalers Inn** is north of the harbor and features Italian dishes.

Charter boats leave the Tides Wharf daily at 7:00 A.M., weather permitting. Call 707-875-3595 for reservations and information on needed gear, bait and license. If you were to catch your limit under the state's sport fishing regulations, you would have 2 salmon, 15 rockcod and 2 lingcod.

Sonoma Coast North

The Sonoma coast, from Bodega Bay to the county line at the Gualala River, is that rare shoreline combination of state beaches, a few towns and, to the north, private lands with limited public access to the sea. Most of it is a dramatic ocean carving of high bluffs and terraces and offshore seastacks that celebrate the incoming tide by sending irregular white plumes into the air. It is a 50-mile spectacle for the visitor who can keep one sure eye on the twists and waves that Highway 1 insists on making all the way north.

From Bodega Bay to Jenner 10 miles away, there are more than a dozen state beaches and campgrounds as well as a succession of overlooks for a quick sea panorama. The Bodega Dunes Campground, part of Sonoma Coast Beach, is just above town, and its 98 campsites for hikers/bikers or sizable trailers are popular year-round. Just beyond, Salmon Creek Beach offers shallow-water swimming at the channel—an exceptional invitation because North Coast beaches are not for swimming. There are no lifeguards and the waters are cold and threatening, with strong currents and backwash. But the walking, sunbathing and beachcombing opportunities seem unlimited. The fishing possibilities are more limited: clams in the mudflats, flatfish at sandy beaches, rockfish and abalone at rocky intertidal areas.

At the Schoolhouse Beach parking lot one midday, I found myself envying the gulls as they soared gracefully off the bluff for a swooping inspection of the surf's edge and the small beach below. It is a steep trail descent to sea level, as it is at neighboring Portugese Beach, Carmet Beach and Colemans Beach. Duncans Landing, five miles north of Bodega Bay, was once a timber shipping point in the 1870s, and you can walk down to the small cove where the loading dock stood. Wright Beach, a mile north, is more accessible and provides campsites and picnic tables. Highway 1 turns inland to cross the Russian River but Sonoma beaches stretch on—Shell Beach, Gull Rock, Blind Beach, Goat Rock. The latter is at the point of a green peninsula at the mouth of the Russian and it offers approaches to both riverside and ocean.

Jenner

The place where a large river empties into the sea can be one of nature's more spectacular gifts, and the one at this small town is enhanced by the steep pitch of the coastline and the great estuarial surge of the waters below. For the northbound motorist, Jenner may seem to come and go quickly: a gas station/grocery, gift shop, small visitor center with picnic ground, a couple of inviting restaurants, the residential section clinging to the hillside. Jenner does have accommodations that give the visitor a chance to appreciate the town's unique location.

I stopped at **River's End Restaurant and Lodge**, also listed as a resort, in Russian River fashion. It sits on a high, hard bend north of the town center and has a few remodeled cabins with ocean views. The one I rented was rustic-pleasant; from its small deck, I watched the low tide and the sunset coincide. Later, the high tide was a welcome interruption from sleep. The restaurant has a reputation with gourmets and an ocean overlook anyone can appreciate. The roadside building began with a general store and tackle shop in 1928; in 1975, the Gramatzki family began to develop the restaurant. German-born Wolfgang Gramatzki, with wide experience as a caterer to the famous, attracts diners with a menu that may offer boneless quail, roast pheasant, homemade spaetzle, Black Forest cherry torte. Each fall he conducts the River's End School of Cooking. Dinner— moderately expensive—is served daily, from early May through September. There are weekend brunches. Call 707–865–2484 for reservations and the off-season schedule. Cabin rates are $50 daily, $225 weekly.

Murphy's Jenner by the Sea has bed & breakfast accommodations, a large restaurant with fireplace lounge, continental cuisine. Weekend rates for suites-with-view are $65 to $90. Rooms are $60. Private homes are available for short-term rental. For reservations, call 707–865–2377.

. . .

Highway 1 becomes an automotive slalom course north of Jenner; if you drive it early morning, keep an eye out for lambs that have strayed downhill and consider the road's edge their own. About three miles north of Jenner, undeveloped Russian Gulch has trails that lead to the beach. The gulch sends the highway on a hairpin course before it straightens on its way to **Fort Ross Historic Park**, a preservation and reconstruction of Russia's major settlement in California.

In 1812, a group of 95 Russians and 40 Aleuts and Kodiak Islanders arrived by Russian-American Fur Company ship and chose this flatland above the sea to build a rectangular fort and village of some 40 buildings. Later viewed as part of the long-held tsarist effort to expand eastward, the outpost served the practical purpose of helping the Russians in their harvest of sea otters and in growing crops for their fur-trading stations in Alaska, which suffered from severe hunger. The 12-foot stockade with its blockhouses was named *Rossiya* for the homeland of the builders.

Today, one of the buildings erected within the fort, the Commandant's House, still stands, following repairs after a fire. Blockhouses and the small Russian Orthodox chapel as well as other structures have been rebuilt to original design. The remaining Commandant's House was the second one built in the fort, apparently to satisfy the needs of the last Russian leader at Ross, Alexander Rotchev, who was a linguist, poet and world traveler. The Russian presence at Fort Ross lasted until 1841, when the scarcity of overhunted sea otters and the failure of the company's shipbuilding efforts led to economic collapse. The enterprising John Sutter, who established Sutter's Fort in the Sacramento Valley, bought the property for $30,000—including 1,700 cattle, 940 horses and mules, a large herd of sheep and a considerable arsenal. Sutter transferred his acquisitions, including some buildings, to the new Sacramento.

Fort Ross State Park, with a picnic area, trails, mini beach, is open 8:00 A.M. to 5:00 P.M. daily. There are weekend guided tours. Admission is $2. Call 707–847–3286 for information.

Privately owned **Timber Cove Campground**, a mile above Ross, occupies a fine coastal sweep. The several facilities include camper hookups, boats and scuba rentals, bait and tackle sales, cabins. Call 707–847–3278 for information. A short distance north, **Stillwater Cove Park** has camping and picnic areas with a $1.50 day-use fee. Camping is $5 for Sonoma residents, $6 for nonresidents. Above the lively cove, abalone fishing regulations are posted to remind divers that the limit is four a day and the minimum size is seven inches. Open seasons are April through June and August through November. Scuba gear is not permitted.

A do-not-disturb-seals warning to visitors explains that pups often appear abandoned on shore but are simply resting while mother is food-shopping. The northern elephant seal, hunted to near extinction by the turn of the century, is now a familiar inhabitant of Northern (and Southern) California waters. But it is vulnerable to the effects of sharing the coastline with man. The California Marine Mammal Center at Marin Headlands in the Bay Area conducts a rescue and care program for stranded mammals. A few years ago at Fort Ross State Park, a bleeding, skin-diseased 200-pound northern elephant seal was taken to the center and treated until it grew to 300 pounds and was able to turn to the ocean again.

Salt Point State Park, 20 miles north of Jenner, covers more than 4,000 acres, oceanside and inland, and provides a choice of beach locations, trails for riding or hiking, campsites. Like many other Sonoma Coast State Beaches, Salt Point is served by the Mendocino Transit Authority coast van. For schedule information and fares, call 707–884–3723 in Ukiah.

I stopped at little **Stump Beach**, a mile away, on a day when the U-shaped cove was sure to add to its heavy collection of timber, logs and nautical accessories. The tide was rising and so was the wind off the sea, and while the little bay had a wild feeling about it, the giant fir trees behind tossed rhythmically in benign contrast. To extend the mood I stopped at neighboring **Fish Mill Cove**—with its familiar state park self-registration (parking $2, dogs 50¢)—and walked one of the trails along the bluff. It was off-season and the sounds and significant movement came from the ocean below. (My car was the only one in the parking area just off Route 1.) It was a day fit for solitary walking, and I eventually crossed the highway and took the entrance road to Kruse Rhododendron State Reserve, about a mile uphill. The reserve is famous for its flowers—California Rose Bay—which begin to bloom in April and continue through June. I was in advance of the early color and also the visitors. I had the Rhododendron Loop Trail and the other well-traveled paths to myself. The great redwoods, the live streams and the evergreen shrubs that would again spread deep rose patches across the forest floor were surroundings enough. Later in the spring, I would see how vividly the rhododendron shows its presence up and down the coast.

For information about the flowering scene at the Kruse State Reserve, call 707–865–2391.

The best-known general store on the Sonoma Coast—perhaps on the entire North Coast—is at **Stewarts Point**, a scattering of houses that give the rocky promontory the appearance of having but recently abandoned the business of shipping lumber. The Stewarts Point Store can supply you with fishing rods, tackle, flour, boots, crackers, wine, newspapers—practically anything else you need to survive on land or sea.

In contrast to this vintage supplier of basics is the long stretch of modern luxury living next door known as **The Sea Ranch**, once part of a 17,500-acre Mexican land grant named Rancho de Herman. As an ambitious second-home colony, The Sea Ranch attracted wide attention and, of course, drew much controversy because of its size and dominant location on the northern edge of the Sonoma Coast. The subdivision's strict building codes, the weathered-timber look of the well-spaced structures that point their wide picture windows to the sea, the posted private roads, inevitably drew approval from planners and buyers and condemnation from those who feared the loss of valuable ocean access. The Sea Ranch has settled into the land and seascape now and an increase in the number of public trails leading to beaches and across the magnificent blufftops has reduced the fortress atmosphere around the development. The public trails, private roads and lands are well-signed. The Sonoma County Parks Department can provide up-to-date information on recently completed access trails.

The Sea Ranch Lodge, located at dramatic Black Point, is an appealing public entree to the ranch community. Its dining room and lounge overlook the bluffs and its secluded rooms are as attractively designed and furnished as they should be to occupy such favored ground. Without thinking about the timing, I checked into the lodge one January Super Bowl weekend and discovered that the environment so overwhelms the athletic spectacle that one easily loses sight of who's playing and what the score is. Since rooms at the lodge are free of both phone and TV, the only place to see the game was on the one set at the bar-lounge. I shared a small table with a young woman from Sebastopol who was drinking herb tea. We were 2 of 22 Super Bowl spectators at this unlikely viewing spot. She

The weathered timber outline of the Sea Ranch Lodge faces the sea at Black Point. It is the center for the controlled Sea Ranch colony.

knew little about football but much about the rewards of walking coastal headlands and what can be observed—the great blue heron on occasion, jack rabbits, the blacktail deer, the variety of seabirds that work the shoreline. She was wearing her blufftop uniform—jeans, a heavy sweater, a wool scarf and walking shoes. She said that she made a weekend habit of driving to the coast on clear, windblown days such as this one. We pooled our pertinent knowledge; I explained a little of the football action on the distant TV and she told me what she had seen before she turned away from the wind to the warmth of a late-afternoon tea. As a hiker of headlands, she clearly was a winner on this Super Bowl Sunday.

Rooms at Sea Ranch Lodge come with custom-made wood furniture, high-angled roof lines, a skylight and corner windows that look toward an old ranch barn, a gray-timbered survivor of Pacific storms. The network of walking trails is just out the door, and you don't need to slide open your windows to hear the constant beat of the surf. Room rates, May through October, start at $81 for a single and run $87 to $125 for a double. Off-season rates are from $71 to $115 (Phone: 707-785-2371). At the north end of the ranch, near the Gualala River, a golf course challenges players with tricky links and winds, and a distracting view from every green.

Sonoma Wine Country

If Napa Valley presents the best and most in American vineyards, its neighbor to the west and north, Sonoma County and the wide-bordered Sonoma Valley, can boast of real diversity in climate and soil and of supplying decisive early history to winemaking in California. Sonoma County sprawls over 1,500 square miles and has a Pacific coastline of 62 miles. Its terrain includes the marshlands of the Petaluma River, the rocky peak of Mt. St. Helena, the erratic course of the Russian River and the unpopulated ridges of the Mendocino Highlands. Wineries, once focused in the valley east of the Sonoma Mountains, have swiftly multiplied around Healdsburg to the north, in the lower Russian River region and in the charming Alexander Valley to the northeast. There are, as they say, now scores of Sonoma wineries—and counting.

Because of its size, Sonoma wine country offers the visitor the chance to walk a headland, canoe a river, hike a park trail and tour a nearby winery. The following consideration of Sonoma wineries is selective and, I hope, provides a cross-section. Guides and maps are easily attainable along the way, but I recommend writing or calling the Sonoma County Economic Development Board for a complimentary map with wineries, parks and campgrounds graphically located: 2300 County Center Drive, Santa Rosa 95401 (Phone: 707–527–2406); or Sonoma County Visitors Bureau, 637 First Street, Santa Rosa 95404 (Phone: 707–545–1420). For a wine and roadmap concentrating on the Sonoma Valley contact Sonoma Valley Chamber of Commerce, 453 First Street East, Sonoma 95476 (Phone: 707–996–1033).

The *Wine Country Review,* distributed free, has maps and directories covering wineries in the Sonoma and Napa valleys plus Lake and Mendocino counties and the North Coast.

Vineyards ready for the harvest stretch up hillsides of the Sonoma Valley. These belong to the modern Kenwood winery.

The Spaniards are credited historically with planting the first grape vines in California but Indian tribes traversing the lush northern valleys may have learned long before that the land and the climate gave life to the small fruit. The Franciscans began the tradition of establishing mission vineyards and wineries at San Diego de Alcala sometime in the 1770s. We know that George Yount took cuttings from General Vallejo's Petaluma Valley vines and began to produce wine near the present Yountville in the 1840s (see pp. 10–11). But a Hungarian nobleman, forced to flee his country for political reasons, is referred to as the state's pioneer viticulturist and the father of California wine. In the 1850s, Count Agoston Haraszthy, experienced in grape cultivation in Europe, came to Sonoma and began developing the existing vineyards at the Buena Vista estate. He is credited with starting the first premium winery there in 1857. Haraszthy later was named Commissioner on the Improvement and Growth of the Grape-vine by the California legislature. As a result of a research tour in Europe, he imported approximately 100,000 vines in hundreds of varieties for distribution in the region. By 1868, about 400,000 vines had been planted in Sonoma County, and Napa Valley soon had more than that number.

Buena Vista The Old Winery Road, curving through tall eucalyptus trees, leads to the historic Haraszthy Cellars on the east side of Sonoma. The vine-covered building faces north, with little exposure to the sun, and the tunnels carved out by Chinese stay at a constant 52° because of their thick limestone insulation. The restored winery serves as Buena Vista's showcase, but it is also a museum in which you can trace the history of winemaking through photographs, a center for Mozart concerts, musical performances by traveling groups such as a German hunting-horn octette and an annual Shakespeare Festival. Buena Vista's working property, planted in the 1970s, is situated in the Carneros region to the south, between the Napa and

Pioneer viticulturist Count Agoston Haraszthy began his development of California grapes here at the Buena Vista cellars in Sonoma.

Sonoma valleys. There Buena Vista harvests over 600 acres in a half-dozen grape varieties. (Phone: 707–938–1266.)

Sebastiani Vineyards Located on Fourth Street East, not far from the town plaza, this was the leading name in winemaking in the Sonoma Valley for decades after Prohibition. The Sebastiani family is probably best known for its hearty bulk reds. Recently, an internal feud resulted in the replacement of the oldest Sebastiani brother at the top of the winery controlled by his mother. The winery has a huge collection of carved wine barrels and casks and also a display of Indian artifacts. (Phone: 707–938–5532.)

Route 12 north from Sonoma brings you close to two small wineries near Jack London's old ranch that can easily be included in a visit to the state park. The **Valley of the Moon Winery**, on Madrone Road just below the Sonoma State Hospital, is run by the Parducci family, whose generations have been producing table wines since the 1940s. Lately, it has made an increase in its more expensive premium offerings. (Phone: 707–996–6941.) Small, new—a first harvest in 1979—**Glen Ellen Winery** is on the Jack London Ranch Road. Tours of the vineyard can be arranged, call 707–996–1066.

Kenwood Vineyards As the Sonoma Highway (12) approaches the community of Kenwood, rows of vines and a road to the right point to this smart, modern winery located where the Pagani Brothers grew grapes in the early years of the century. The Lee family is responsible for the revamping and for the steady rise in attention given their premium varietals. Sales and tasting facilities are in an attractive hillside building. (Phone: 707–833–5891.)

Château St. Jean Just beyond the Kenwood Post Office on the left of Route 12 and before Adobe Canyon Road leads right to Sugarloaf Ridge State Park, a sign directs one to this imposing winery installation. Château St. Jean has been making sparkling wines since 1980 at its facility at Graton, above Sebastopol, but its excellent table wines are processed here. Fruit comes from the 70-plus surrounding vineyards or is supplied by near growers. The winery made an impact on critics and vineyardists with its Chardonnays of the mid-1970s and impresses new visitors with its business complex here. The wine-tasting and retail sales are located in a residential château, and the picnic table and sitting area is carefully landscaped. The up-to-date winery is open for self-guided tours, a real reward if you have grown impatient after tagging along with scheduled tour groups. The grape-crushing space with large stainless steel fermenting tanks provides a pleasing assault on the sense of smell; the French Nevers and Limousin oak barrels, when examined closely, make the aging process seem an impressively rich part of winemaking. I particularly recommend a good look at the display on cooperage. Your own tour should end with a climb to the top of the tower at the winery where, from the balcony, the view of the immaculate plant, the graceful château and the long stretch of vineyards to the west brings a wine-haze fantasy of being cellarmaster just for one day. (Phone 707–833–4134.)

Wine tourers are attracted to the top of the tower at Château St. Jean after a sampling of Chardonnay or a sparkling wine.

Healdsburg, which for years was the center for the growers of grapes, apples, pears, prunes, cherries and hops, now turns to nearby vineyards for its economic outlook. The grape trade, big in the Healdsburg area even through Prohibition times, is a dominant factor today. Within a short radius, including Alexander Valley and the Dry Creek area, there are some two dozen wineries, many of them young enough to have made their first crush in the late 1970s. Healdsburg is physically attached to the curving Russian River, but the influential vineyards spread across a more varied terrain.

Clos du Bois A good proof of the caution that the appearance of the winery does not necessarily reflect the bouquet of the wine. Clos du Bois, founded in 1964, is located in a shedlike building or two in downtown Healdsburg at 5 Fitch Street, hard by the Northwestern Pacific tracks and the town's abandoned railroad depot. The facility includes cellars, oak barrel storage, holding tanks and an adequate tasting area. The vineyards are at a distance: about 500 acres in the Alexander Valley and 70 in Dry Creek. Production is geared to expand to 140,000 cases. Its list of seven varietals includes highly recommended Gerwürztraminer and a proprietor's reserve Cabernet Sauvignon. (Phone: 707-433-5576.)

Mill Creek Vineyards Just outside Healdsburg proper on the Westside Road, which threads through the Russian River Valley, an attractively designed redwood structure atop a knoll of land identifies this small family winery. Charles Kreck and sons Bob and Bill began their vineyard operation in 1975, the two-story tasting and sales facility, built mostly with redwood from the Kreck ranch, was completed in 1982. It includes a large picnic deck overlooking the valley, ideal for drinking one of the eight wines produced by Mill Creek. The mill pond nearby has a working wheel.

Simi To the north of Healdsburg, this winery with a lengthy past attracts a procession of visitors. Simi's famous hand-hewn stone structure was built by Pietro and Giuseppe Simi in 1890, and members of the family continued to be involved in wine-making until 1970. Simi suffered along with other Healdsburg area wineries during Prohibition; yet some managed to prosper on one or the other side of the law. On Healdsburg Avenue, not far from Simi, the old Olivetto Winery building stands, some locals say, as a monument to the making of "jackass whiskey."

A wooden bridge leads to the hand-hewn stone winery building of Simi in Healdsburg built in 1890 by Italian immigrants.

Simi more recently went through another period of decline before it was acquired by Moët-Hennessy and was decisively reequipped and given expanded goals under winemaker Zelma Long in 1979. Simi's tasting room and garden picnic area are located just off Healdsburg Avenue. The impressive, long-standing winery—restored and modernized within—is across a bridge and the railroad link to nearby Boise-Cascade. (Phone: 707-433-6981.)

To expand your acquaintance with the river-divided Alexander Valley after tasting the wines made from grapes of the region, there are two wineries worth visiting: On Route 128 South, take the Alexander Valley Road leading from Healdsburg Avenue to **Alexander Valley Vineyards**, which is located on the original homesite of Cyrus Alexander, whose cattle once dominated the landscape. The Wetzel family has, since 1975, been producing estate-bottled wines at this pleasant site. (Phone: 707-433-7209.) A short distance south on 128, **Field Stone** offers the chance to examine the only underground winery built in California in this century. The winery was the 1976 creation of the late Wallace Johnson, who gets credit for inventing—and putting to use here —the mechanical grape harvester. Field Stone has a bucolic picnic area under fine oak trees on a slope above the wine cellar. (Phone: 707-433-7266.)

The northern expression of Sonoma County wineries can be seen by using less speed and more attention as you drive 101 and approach Geyserville. The kiln-styled towers of **Souverain Cellars** are visible on the left and are reached by taking the Independence Lane Exit. Part of a growers' association which uses grapes from several Northern California vineyards, Souverain has released its own estate-bottled wines. A restaurant and scheduled entertainments add to this 1973 winery's tourist popularity. (Phone: 707-433-8281.) On the opposite side of the highway, **Trentadue Winery**, named for its veteran wine-producing owner, sells a variety of reasonably priced wines. Visitors sit at outdoor tables protected from the valley sun by a grape arbor. (Phone: 707-433-3104.)

Geyser Peak   The winery with a well-known name dates to 1880 when Augustus Quitzow came to the area for mineral water benefits and decided it was an ideal place to grow grapes. The restored winery occupies a hillside on Chianti Road at the north end of Geyserville (Exit 101 on Canyon Road). An appealing vine-covered facility to visit, Geyser Peak has both walking trails and picnic grounds. It has trimmed its large production to focus more on premium wines. Its ranches are located in Alexander Valley and to the south in the Carneros region. (Phone: 707-433-6585.)

J. Pedroncelli Winery   Family-run, as it was when it was started in the late 1920s, this small, old-look winery is near

The renovated winery reveals modern angles but Geyser Peak has been producing wines at the northern side of Geyserville since 1880.

Geyser Peak on Canyon Road. Pedroncelli has developed a line of affordable and dependable table wines. (Phone: 707–857–3531.)

Five miles above Geyserville, Asti was settled by Italians and Swiss from San Francisco in the 1880s for the commercial—and social—purpose of making wines. From that agricultural cooperative, named for Asti in Northern Italy, came the famous name **Italian Swiss Colony**. Its inexpensive wines were shipped from the winery in railroad tank cars all over the country, and its premiums won awards abroad. But in the 1970s, Colony, run by a business conglomerate, went into economic decline. When it was forced to shut its doors to the public, many vineyard owners in Northern California were shocked. Reorganized in 1983, Colony again opened its tasting room—said to be the oldest in the United States—and the large picnic area, formal gardens and regular tours remain popular with visitors. (Phone: 707–433–2333.) Also located in historic Asti is the tasting room and retail outlet of **Pat Paulsen Vineyards**. The entertainer planted his first vines in 1971 and built a winery eight years later. (Phone: 707–894–3197.)

Pastori Winery   The unglamorous, laborious, old-school side of winemaking in Northern California is in evidence at this modest winery, about halfway between Geyserville and Asti. The facility and surrounding vineyards can be seen from 101 and reached on parallel Geyserville Avenue. The old ranch barns are protected with sheet metal and heavily insulated to serve as the wine cellar. Frank Pastori runs the winery, harvests the 64 acres of vines and fruit trees, does his own limited bottling. His wife Edith most often looks after the small tasting and sales room. Pastori wines, which include a fine Zinfandel and a Cabernet Sauvignon of modest price, are sold only here. Like many other little vineyard proprietors, Pastori sells grapes to larger wineries and crushes grapes on order.

Field Stone adapted the idea of wine caves to build this unique underground winery on a pleasant hillside in the Alexander Valley.

Pastori's father, Constante, came from Italy to grow grapes in upper Sonoma County in 1914. Prohibition and World War II caused closings of the winery, but Frank started production again in 1972 after working and learning at the nearby Nervo vineyards established in 1888. I asked him if he had any desire to expand now that he had secured a reputation for quality.

"It's a huge next step," he said. "You need a staff, you need sales reps. You get a call from LA or San Francisco, and they want you at a wine-tasting—if you say no, you don't have the time, it gets around. I do well selling to the local trade and to other wineries. I'd rather stay small and close to this place."

He thinks that one of the problems established vineyard owners face today was caused by the too-rapid expansion of small wineries. "Why, the price per acre shot up to $20,000!" He says the price of American wines when compared with foreign imports is now too high to allow for much consumer growth.

"In 1985," he continued "a lot of guys had to leave their grapes on the vine because there was no home for them. Gallo is more careful about who they buy from—and they're the biggest buyer around. But now they've got their own huge ranch in the Dry Creek area." He laughed and went on, "This business is full of trends. White Zinfandel is the hottest thing on the market now. But you have to bet there'll be too much White Zinfandel around soon."

The reopening of Colony up the road had helped him, he admitted. "People going to Asti see my building and sign and stop in." The door to the tasting room had been locked while he took care of a vineyard chore, and he opened it. The interior was pleasantly cool and uncomplicated—like the glass of Cabernet he poured. I complimented him. The place wasn't very fancy, he said, but it was practical. "I've had three people stop by today, and two of them bought a case!" Winemaking on a family scale has its own small rewards.

Frank or Edith Pastori can be reached at 707–857–3418.

MENDOCINO
COUNTY

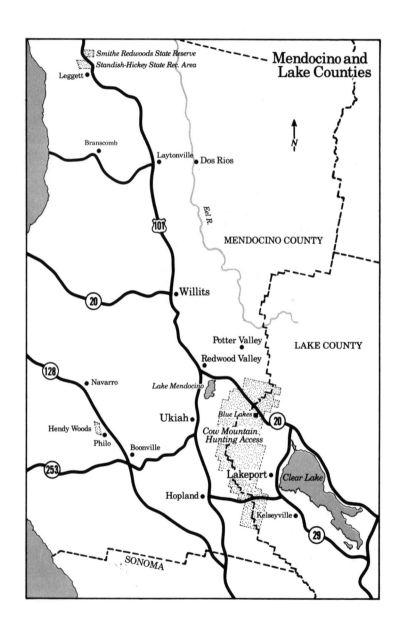

Smithe Redwoods State Reserve
Standish-Hickey State Rec. Area

Leggett

Branscomb

Laytonville • Dos Rios

Eel R.

101

MENDOCINO COUNTY

N

•Willits

20

Potter Valley

LAKE COUNTY

Redwood Valley

128

• Navarro

Lake Mendocino

Ukiah •

Blue Lakes

20

Hendy Woods

Cow Mountain
Hunting Access

Philo

Boonville

Clear Lake

253

Lakeport •

Hopland •

Kelseyville •

29

SONOMA

Mendocino and
Lake Counties

Hopland

A RIVER (Russian) runs by it and so does a railroad (Northwestern Pacific), and it is connected to Routes 101 and 175 (to Lakeport and Kelseyville) and the old East Side Road to Talmage. Because of its location, Hopland survived the decline and virtual disappearance of the beer hops industry that gave it a name by pruning newly developed vineyards and fruit trees and encouraging tourists to stop for food or drink. Hopland's population of approximately 1,000 is augmented on weekends by young people who count it a pleasantly situated oasis, home of wineries, a brewery-pub and a new-old hotel.

Hopland sits in the rich valley of Rancho de Sanel, as it was once known, and it is surrounded by ranches including the huge Crawford Ranch on Crawford Creek and the Pratt Ranch to the east. Nearby the Nacomis Indian Rancheria reaches into the Mayacamas foothills. For years, Indian families from the rancheria joined migratory workers as hop pickers in fields first planted in the 1850s. The landscape around Hopland was marked by numerous drying kilns, like so many silos, in which the hops were treated over wood fires.

One of the Indian hop pickers from the rancheria, Elsie Allen, describes in her book *Pomo Basketweaving* the struggle of her people during the early years of the century, as they battled epidemic illness and eked out a living in the hop fields and at sheepshearing or woodcutting on ranches. At age 62, she finally realized a personal—and tribal—success: "I found the time I was seeking to start my basketweaving again. I went out and dug the roots and gathered the willows and hunted around for the beautiful twigs of redbud myself. I have been able to create many fine baskets from those, as small as a dime up to large storage baskets and including some of the famous feather baskets that made the Pomos renowned. There is a rich and beautiful feeling to have these useful and lovely baskets grow into being under the work of your own hands and the designs that grow with them. From 1969 to 1971 I finished fifty-four baskets."

As the Pomo basketmaking craft was revived in the Hopland area, so, in a fashion, was the beer hops business. In 1983, a new microbrewery (production less than 10,000 barrels) opened in town, an enterprise that developed out of the reputation home brewers Michael Laybourn and Norman Franks acquired for the product they called Thunder Beer. The **Mendocino Brewing Company** (tavern and beer garden and restaurant attached)—or simply the Hopland Brewery—is in the easily located heart of Hopland on Route 101. Look for the brewhouse, designed as an old hop kiln with cupola, a replica of the ubiquitous kilns that accompanied the cultivation of hops in pre-Prohibition times. When I last stopped for a brew, the Hopland was retailing all of its production from the tavern, a brick structure that once housed the town's post office, but there were plans for future distribution of bottles and kegs in the state. I lean toward a mug (10 ounces) of Red Tail Ale, a touch heavier than the Peregrine Pale Ale and lighter than the Black Hawk Stout. The Red Tail, 5% alcohol, is available in take-home, returnable 51-ounce bottles. A Red Tail mug or two may encourage you to try a hot sausage or a burger at the moderately priced brewery restaurant.

Hopland offers a choice for wine-tasters and winery-tourers. The extremely productive **Fetzer Winery**, with vineyards in Redwood Valley, was started by Oregon lumberman Bernard Fetzer in 1968; it has a tasting room in a restaurant-gallery complex in town. The Fetzer operation, with more than 3,000 acres in Mendocino County, is run by 10 Fetzer children. **McDowell Valley Vineyards**, which uses integrated solar systems in its production, occupies long-established growing lands east of

Hopland on Route 175. The small **Milano Winery**, south on 101, made its first crush in former hop kilns in 1978. **Estate William Baccala**, north of Hopland on 101, offers wine-tasting in a nineteenth-century ranch house.

On a sparkling winter afternoon in Hopland, I found myself unexpectedly wine-tasting at the bar at **Thatcher's**, "The Hotel at Hopland," where the barmaid was trying to make a choice among Chardonnays being promoted by a traveling wine salesman. "When it comes to sampling wines," the barmaid explained, "I'm like a kid in an ice cream parlor. I like all flavors." After volunteering my choice, I arrived easily at the decision to stay overnight at the recently renovated hotel, a rambling Victorian structure that dates back to the 1890s. It is one of Hopland's oldest. Because it was midweek and off-season I was given three or four keys and told to make a room choice up the angled staircase. The renovated rooms are named after old Hopland families, and I chose the Albert Room, complete with woodframed pictures of Alberts on the wall. There was a settee, a brass bed, plants on a marble-top table, a fan in the 12-foot ceiling, and a bathroom with claw-foot tub, more spacious than most rooms I have occupied.

Dinner was served near a wood-crackling fireplace, and the grilled red snapper came attractively garnished with grapes,

It was at the beginning—1890—the plain old Hopland Hotel and after many changes of style and owners it marks the heart of a brewery town.

pears and orange slices. The maitre d' gave both the fireplace and my table attention enough. I admired the 14-foot ceiling in the room, but he said it did present a cobweb-reaching problem. To boost weekend business, Thatcher's was trying live music and occasional dinner theatre. The bar in the new-old lobby was booming when I returned to the ghosts of the Albert family upstairs for some easily acquired sleep.

I learned months later that my overnight in Hopland was but another historic episode in the uneven life of the old hotel. It had closed, temporarily, and was again in search of new proprietors.

At the junction of 101 and 175 in Hopland, a county route—the Mt. House Road—provides an eight-mile connector to Route 128 that leads to Boonville, the lovely Anderson Valley and the coast. Because of its well-paved winding way through ranchlands dotted with live oaks, I like to use the Mt. House Road as a scenic detour en route to or from Cloverdale and Geyserville. It is relatively traffic free and treats you to one of those small, ideally situated Mendocino valleys as the road dips down to cross Cummiskey Creek.

Ukiah

Ukiah can be bypassed, more or less, by holding to north-south Highway 101, but consider it a motorist's mistake not to take an easy exit and turn into town. Ukiah is the Mendocino County seat and its largest community—approaching 14,000—and it is pleasantly placed on the sloping western side of the Yokaya Valley, made wide by the Russian River. Yokaya is Indian for deep valley, and the Yokaya (or Yokayo) grant eventually gave birth to the town whose name evolved to Ukia and then to its present spelling. Sam Lowry was apparently the first white settler to build a cabin (1856), and three years later the place was chosen as county seat—succeeding administration by neighboring Sonoma County.

When the valley was more prominently occupied by crops than people, Ukiah was a big producer of pears, prunes and hops and was a livestock center that boasted the Ukiah Rodeo. The fields of hops have given way to grapes, and although there are orchards heavy with fruit, three times as many workers are employed in such local industries as the Masonite Corporation and the Louisiana-Pacific sawmill as in agriculture.

Ukiah's mountain-framed location and its wide-street look suggest that it is an appealing place to live. On South Dora Street, parallel to State Street, the most generous bike lane any cyclist could hope for gives the visitor the impression that Ukiah has its priorities in order. The town park, at the residential western edge, includes a hilly, par-70, 18-hole municipal golf course and a ball park immaculately maintained and scenically laid out beneath Lookout Peak. The green-covered grandstand of Anton Stadium speaks for Ukiah's long enthusiasm for baseball. In the early decades of the century, local youths picked hops on nearby ranches during the week and played highly competitive ball on weekends against such arch rivals as Willits, Boonville, and Fort Bragg and occasionally against professional teams that traveled all the way from the Bay Area. When Ukiah faced Fort Bragg away, it took four hours to make the trip over the coastal ridge by the Orr Springs Road. Spirited ballgames are still played at picturesque Anton Stadium; in the fall, the field is used for high school football.

Ukiah is municipally short of historic landmarks, but a visit to the redwood Sun House, the former home of artist Grace Carpenter Hudson and her historian husband John Hudson, will provide a worthwhile introduction to Pomo Indian culture. Located in downtown Ukiah, the Sun House is open to the public Wednesday through Saturday afternoons. Railroad buffs might want to stop at Ukiah's bright-white depot, Milepost 114 on the Northwestern Pacific Railroad, which carries freight from Eureka (Milepost 284) south to San Raphael and Sebastini. Ukiah is not famous for its indigenous cuisine or quaint lodging facilities. It offers a small-city quota of motels; the **Western Traveler** on South Orchard, near Route 101, is both convenient and economical. Nearby on South State Street, **The Green Barn** restaurant pulls a steady crowd of local bar and dinner customers.

Just east of Ukiah, across the Russian River, the small town of Talmage was once populated by those who worked for the large state mental hospital. Talmage remains a residential extension of Ukiah, but the hospital has closed and it is now "The City of Ten Thousand Buddhas," with a monastery and Buddhist university occupying the institutional buildings. The Dharma Realm chose its site well. Behind it a small road, jeep trails and firebreaks find their way up Cow Mountain Ridge to the hunting access beyond.

Ukiah's major recreation area, Lake Mendocino, lies just north of the city. A three-mile stretch of water, it was created with the completion of the Coyote Dam by the Army Corps of Engineers in 1958. The well-groomed surroundings are covered with campsites and picnic grounds, and the lakefront is equipped with launching ramps, boat rental and fishing tackle outlets and a stretch of bathing beach.

Route 20, which provides access to the north end of busy Lake Mendocino, leads to the pleasant rural sides of Potter Valley cut by the east fork of the Russian River. The Indians who once dominated the valley were rounded up and taken to the large reservation near Covello in upper Mendocino County. Some rebelled at the forced resettling and slipped back to their former dwelling places. Descendants of these Indians may be found in small rancherias—encampments that became sanctioned by the Department of Interior's Bureau of Indian Affairs and held in trust status—in Potter Valley, nearby Redwood Valley and at the edge of Ukiah on the Orr Springs Road.

When the Potter Valley Irrigation Canal was completed, tap-

The ornate entrance to the City of Ten Thousand Buddhas in Talmage marks the site of a discontinued state mental hospital.

ping Eel River waters, the ranches that had been devoted to wheat, hogs and cattle were able to develop orchards and fields that produce pears, berries, melons and vegetables. The productive valley is only about seven-miles long; the village center of Potter Valley is 10 miles above Ukiah. If you extend the drive over the mountains to the northeast, you are rewarded by the sight of Lake Pillsbury, the large power and irrigation project that began in 1921 with the construction of Scott Dam on the free-flowing Eel. The reservoir surface is over 2,000 acres, and the waters are stocked with trout and bluegill. There is a choice of campgrounds and resorts, and a road runs along Horsepasture Gulch toward the distant Hull Mountain lookout at an elevation of 6,873 feet. The peak looks over Lake County's state game refuge, where elk have been reintroduced, and the huge Mendocino National Forest.

Willits

Before starting the climb from Ukiah to its upcounty neighbor, Willits, 25-miles away, there is the opportunity to visit old-name wineries on the north side of town. The modern facility of **Cresta Blanca** is operated by the pre-Prohibition winery of that name in Livermore, California, and is one of the largest in the area. **Parducci Wine Cellars**, on Parducci Road off North Main Street, was selling wines of distinction well before Mendocino County was on the wine map. Adolph Parducci planted his vineyards in the early 1930s and much of the wine, now produced by Parducci sons, comes from these local vines and others located around Talmage. The family-operated **Weibel Champagne Vineyards**, founded by a Swiss winemaker at Mission San Jose, has a tasting room just off North Main Street, easily identified by the large inverted champagne glass on its roof design.

Route 101 sweeps upward to a summit of 1,956 feet, where you are likely to see logging trucks pulled over for a break at the fuel stop and a small grocery-deli. Ridges to the west do not boast impressive elevations, but both Impassable Rocks and Irene Peak have a formidable look. The steady grind of highway traffic does not discourage the white deer—originally acquired from William Randolph Hearst's San Simeon ranch—from making occasional appearances along nearby slopes. The highway drops quickly and narrows noticeably in its approach to Willits, which occupies a smaller basin—Little Lake Valley—than does Ukiah.

It also presents a more rustic visage, fitting for an old timber town that enjoys celebrating its lawless past. Black Bart, the famous robber of stage coaches, is something of a local hero. The feud between the Coates and Frost families, less famous than the ill-will expressed by the Hatfields and McCoys but very deadly indeed (six killed and three wounded in an 1867 shootout), is reviewed for historical society members. Willits's Fourth of July rodeo and community carnival, held since the 1920s at the Frontier Rodeo Grounds on the east side of town, is one of California's longest-running riding, roping and racing shows. Willits is the eastern terminus of the popular tourist railway,

The Skunk Line train carries tourists over the coastal ridge, Willits to Fort Bragg and back, on a rugged old logging route.

the California Western's "Skunk" line, which started as a log carrier in the 1800s.

Willits was once Willitsville in recognition of early settler and storekeeper Hiram Willits, who had forsaken Indiana in a quest for California gold. Perhaps the town should have been renamed Bartsville in honor of the highwayman who operated in the vicinity from the mid-1870s until 1883, when capture and a prison term at San Quentin halted his successful career. Black Bart left behind a legend that resulted in a commemorative Black Bart Rock (one of his professional hiding places) south of Willits. Five miles outside town, at the summit of U.S. 101, the **Ridge** motel-restaurant invites people to eat in the Black Bart Dining Room and drink in the Black Bart Saloon.

Black Bart qualifies as an acceptable civic hero because of his reputation as a gentleman brigand. His real name was Charles C. Bolton, and he traveled on foot and alone and struck with éclat, wearing a mask and a linen duster. Mr. Bolton was not one to dry-gulch stage drivers who had forced their team to make the hard mountain climb from Ukiah. He was, according to many victims of his 27 stage holdups, invariably polite while performing his criminal handiwork. After relieving Wells Fargo of its valuables, he usually left a satirical rhyme and his signature—"Black Bart, Po-8." Willits happily claims him, but he ranged wide through the Sierra and the coastal high country. When he was traced and finally captured in San Francisco, it was discovered that Mr. Bolton had a legitimate cover as a mining engineer.

I have found that a rewarding way to spend a few hours in Willits is to combine a visit to the town's tree-shaded Grove Recreation Area on East Commercial Street with a tour of the **Mendocino County Museum** close by, open days, Wednesday through Sunday. The Grove is a fine picnic space at offbeat hours and the South Main Deli is the choice for a well-constructed sandwich, a salad and a beverage. Like any deli with a solid local reputation, it gets frantic at the lunch break.

The wood-framed, two-story museum, built with funds from the Mendocino County Historical Society in 1972, contains artifacts of life in the area from Indian times through pioneer and contemporary periods. For a first-time visitor, it provides a quick visual course in area history. The museum is best known for its permanent collection of Pomo Indian baskets and other Native American crafts. Among the impressive works of basket art is one by Nellie White, a Central Pomo, made at the Yokaya Rancheria about 1930. It has a foundation of willow shoots, its serving strands are of split roots and sedge, the design of split roots and bulrush. On the label is the basketweaver's comment: "This has got the black root."

Many of the quotes accompanying the artifacts in the museum are from *Mendocino County Remembered*, the oral history prepared for the county's American Bicentennial History Project, and they add a pungent personality you don't encounter in many museum labels. A photograph of the small coastal town of Albion during its boom sawmill years carries the obituary: "I remember what Albion was like. . . . Albion went kaplooey in 1926 or 1927."

Exhibits include a giant redwood stump and the awesome tools of the lumberjacks: a great crosscut saw, a severe-looking single-bitted axe. A replica of a tanbark mule bearing a heavy load stands in a lifelike salute to the county's once-thriving tanbark industry. An 1874 prophecy of how Mendocino would be transformed by its environment and its vast crop of oaks and sequoias belongs to Walt Whitman as displayed in the museum: "The chorus and indications / the vistas of / coming humanity / the settlements, features all / In the Mendocino woods I caught."

There is no counting the tourists who come to Willits and miss the Mendocino County Museum but catch one of the "Skunk" trains, which depart from the California Western Depot, an easy stroll down East Commercial Street. A public relations consultant could not have chosen a more unlikely and unforgettable nickname for a scenic railway. It dates back to the mid-1920s when the CWR introduced a railbus made by truck manufacturer Mack International. The self-propelled, single-car "train" carried baggage and people to and from Willits and Fort Bragg. As it labored along the twisting ridge route, the rail bus released gas fumes that announced the CWR's approach long before it became visible. A conductor is credited with naming the train. Some people say the train actually looked skunk-like when compared to the steam locomotives that had hauled passengers since 1904. The original "Skunk" railbus was mortally damaged in 1964 in a collision with a train powered by a diesel, which the CWR then used for most service.

The "Skunk's" route is 40 miles, Willits to Fort Bragg, and the tracks cross 31 bridges and trestles and pass through two major tunnels. A one-way journey takes about three and a half hours, with stops along the way, regular and irregular. After some abrupt horseshoeing beyond the 1,700-foot tunnel west of Willits, the train follows the Noyo River Valley toward the sea, passing such notable place-names as Shake City, Irmulco,

Northspur, Olde Camp Seven, Grove Junction. (In the summer it is possible to shorten the trip by changing trains at Northspur and returning to Willits. The same choice can be made on an eastbound trip from Fort Bragg.)

Normal equipment on trains during the high season includes coaches and an open observation car. Most winter service is provided by a modern yellow model of the self-propelled "Skunk" car. Like any scenic railway, the CWR trains do get crowded with families and vocal observation-car passengers pointing and picture snapping at every bend in the line. In the off-season you may have a better opportunity to observe the high redwood country and to check the farmers, hunters and adventurers who depart quietly at no-name junctions. But you must allow for a schedule that does not provide a return train —Willits or Fort Bragg—until the next day. One-way fares are $12 for adults, $6 for children; roundtrip, $16 and $8. Phone 707–964–6371 for reservations and information.

MENDOCINO COAST

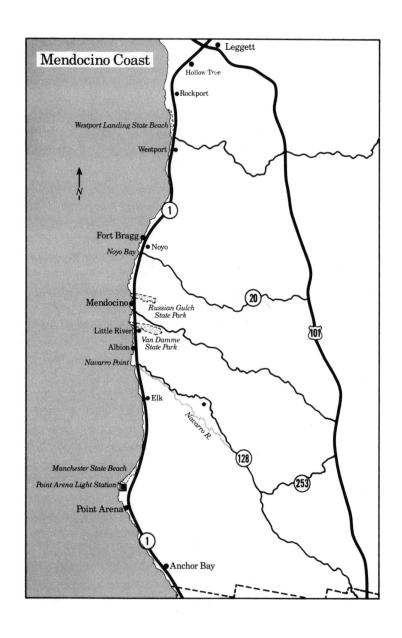

Mendocino Coast

Leggett

Hollow Tree

Rockport

Westport Landing State Beach

Westport

N

① 1

Fort Bragg
Noyo
Noyo Bay

Mendocino
Russian Gulch
State Park

Little River
Van Damme
State Park
Albion

Navarro Point

Elk

Navarro R.

② 20

⑫8 128

⑩1 101

②53 253

Manchester State Beach

Point Arena Light Station

Point Arena

① 1

Anchor Bay

Gualala

Halfway across the Gualala River Bridge, driving north, you pass the Mendocino County marker and enter a coastline characterized by small former lumbering towns, more sheer-cut headlands and rugged offshore seastacks. To the east, rivers, creeks, and serpentine roads reach down from forested ridges. It is, of course, a dramatic, jagged extension of the Sonoma shoreline.

The first conversation I had in Gualala (pronounced Wah-la-la, to approximate the Indian term for the meeting of waters) was, appropriately, with two fishermen at the old (1903) Gualala Hotel, its wide veranda, balcony and high-ceilinged public rooms restored by new owners. They had given up the pursuit of steelhead trout for the day and were anxious to talk, not about the one that got away but about the one the sea lion caught.

"He came right up the river a good half mile. There wasn't much left of the fish, I tell you." They felt that sea lions had legitimate fishing rights at the river's mouth but that steelhead were hard enough to catch on their migration without such bold competition. The Gualala, a popular steelhead fishing water from December through February, has a wide south fork that parallels the Pacific for a couple of miles. Gualala Point Regional Park occupied the point of land and has freshwater swimming. The park also reaches to the ocean.

There are several motels and inns, besides the classic old **Gualala Hotel**, along the coast to nearby Anchor Bay. The **Surf Motel** and the **North Coast Inn** are located in town. The **Old Milano Hotel**, opened as a hotel/pub in 1905, and the

High bluffs, soaring seabirds, the restless ocean are all part of the timeless scene along the Sonoma and Mendocino coasts.

Whale Watch Inn by the Sea have adults-only bed & breakfast accommodations. The Anchor Bay area becomes busy with realty-sales signs and traffic to and from the privately operated campground, with its trailer hookup, at Fish Rock Beach. The beach remains open all year and caters to fishing enthusiasts.

Along the ridge above Highway 1 as it hugs the coast, the old stage route, now called Ten Mile Road, runs between Gualala and Point Arena. Actually the stage road is 16-plus miles between the points; the coastal highway is just over 14 miles. South of Point Arena the *Moat Creek Access,* which once carried the more colorful name of Whiskey Shoals, attracts divers and fishermen to its tidal pools.

Point Arena

In the lumbering boom days, Point Arena was one of the busiest ports on the North Coast. Steam schooners, the *Sea Foam,* the *Point Arena,* and the *Pomo* among others, carried passengers and freight overnight to and from San Francisco. Business buildings, hotels and saloons lined the sloping main street and some that survived the 1906 earthquake and fire remain today, even though commerce and population are both fractions of what the town used to have.

In the oral history *Mendocino Remembered,* Chester Bishop, born in 1896, says, "I knew three or four guys got killed there in Point Arena. Shot. . . . Well, it was a rough place. There was thirteen saloons there and three or four hotels. There was the Grand Hotel, the Point Arena Hotel, a Finnish hotel and then the Italian hotel. People drank. Fourth of July was a big time. All these guys came from out in the woods. . . . They'd stay two or three weeks. They'd just lay around and drink and get drunk."

Point Arena's rollicking times faded with the timber and tanbark trade, but it remained prominent on the map because of the Point Arena Light Station, reached by taking Lighthouse Road off Highway 1 and heading for its white silhouette. The light began its service to ships in 1870; when the 1906 earthquake hit this coastal area with disastrous effect, the brick tower and lens were badly damaged. The rebuilt tower of reinforced concrete stands 115-feet high and is considered 'quakeproof. The light has signaled automatically since 1976, but visitors can climb the winding iron stairs and inspect the original two-ton Fresnel lens with its hand-fashioned, cut-glass prisms. The view from the top is awesome.

I paid the $1 admission fee (hours: 11:00 A.M.—2:30 P.M. daily) and took the 147 steps, which I counted in hopes of shortening the ascent. A guide at the beacon level suggested that I catch my breath by searching for whales off the distant buoy. She said that they had been coming by in twos and threes for over an hour. But after a long, easy-breathing vigil, I settled for the remarkable sight of a sunlit, quiet sea and the long march of coastline south toward Sea Lion Rocks and north to Manchester Beach and beyond. If you are going to get shut out on a whale watch, the top of Point Arena Light is a most agreeable place to accept defeat.

The **Garcia River** arrives at the ocean east of the lighthouse peninsula, and in the winter you can see the whistling swans— or tundra swans—who come from the Arctic to occupy the flood-

Point Arena Light has given historic service to coastal shipping. Rebuilt after the 1906 earthquake, it now offers automated guidance.

plain. Miner Hole Road, off 1, leads to the Garcia River Access.

Manchester Beach State Park is my choice as the beach to get lost on during the months of late fall or early spring—even in the cool of winter. Beach and seagrass-covered dunes spread over 970 acres, and there are standard campgrounds and environmental and group campsites. The beach itself is magnificent in size and in its appearance as the coastline's major driftwood graveyard. Giant redwood logs from distant rivers lie on shore, providing fine windbreaks or privacy or—as small pieces with burnt butt ends indicate, fuel for warming beach fires. I have been to Manchester when the few other beach-goers were tiny figures shimmering distances away, but I have never felt lonely. The wind, the heaping driftwood, the swirling beachgrass prevent that. At such times, it can be a wild and restoring place.

At the road's turn near one of the small beach parking areas, a fenced-in building holds the Point Arena Undersea Cable installation "providing telephone communications to Hawaii and the Far East." At the nearby camping section a sign says, "Each campsite consists of cleared area that will accommodate a tent, picnic table and metal fire ring." The service area has a large water tank and "two unisex Shasta-type self-composting toilets." Campers can gather firewood west of the duneline (vegetation area) and are warned that beach campsites are subject to high northwest winds during summer months. Regular campsites are $3 overnight; environmental campsites are $6. (Phone: 707-937-5804.)

You pass a familiar Route 1 sign just before the Manchester Beach turn: "Winding road next 21 miles. Watch out for bicycles." Soon you are encountering the triangular speed warnings of 20 mph. "Bluffing it" safely on Highway 1 is a matter of swinging into the rhythm of taking the sharp left that threatens to send you soaring off the bluff and into the waiting surf and *thinking* about the equally sharp right that quickly follows. It is useful to adjust to the idea that the glow of sunshine on your shoulder will be eye-blinding about 100 yards down or up the road. To be intimidated by trucks, fore or aft, is the coward's way; to give them their share of the road and a log size more is the prudent course. I like Highway 1, from Bodega Bay all the way to Leggett. It is as far removed from a drag strip as a road can be.

The town of **Elk** is strung shortly along tall bluffs about halfway between Manchester and Mendocino. From a small parking place, a path drops to the state beach below, skirting posted private property. Elk looks down on seastacks where timber ships once maneuvered to the loading trestle for their haul of lumber from local mills. Logs arrived from the interior on the Greenwood Creek and the Elk Creek railroads. Elk, known as Greenwood until it became confused with another California town of the same name, closed its lumbering operations in 1932. But it was once alive with millhands, railroad workers, wagon drivers, mule skinners and, occasionally, celebrities like Jack London, who must have observed a useful scene or two in the boisterous, elk-horned saloon of the Union Hotel.

Albion

Albion, six miles north, has a thriving mill town past similar to that of Elk. A river runs through it, although not as impressive as the nearby Navarro River, which Route 128 follows south-eastward through the long Anderson Valley. The Albion River cuts a deep cove at the sea, crossed by Highway 1 on a wooden and steel-fortified trestle bridge. On the flats below, a private campground and small marina are located near the site of the once-dominant sawmill company with lumber-drying kilns that spread toward the wharf. Albion's first sawmill, in 1854, was a revolutionary steam-powered sash saw that had a capacity of 4,000 feet of lumber a day. It was destroyed by fire, as were the next three mills built, giving Albion a reputation as being either a hard-luck or a hard-case town. When the fifth mill was built in 1902, it was described as "one of the best organized, most efficient lumber operations on the West Coast." The lumber trade ended in Albion in 1928.

The town lingers and so does its name, as poetic as any on the coast. The first white landholder in the area was English-born William Anthony Richardson. A man of the seven seas, he became a Captain of the Port of San Francisco and married the daughter of the Mexican commander of the Presidio. When he received his land grant in 1844, which included 10,520 acres of coast and timberland, the rancho was given the Celtic name of his homeland, Albion.

On the north side of the high trestle bridge, the **Albion River Inn** gives the town the distinction of having one of the finest seafood restaurants on the Mendocino coast. The inn is an un-pretentious, low building surrounded by flowers and fronted with windows that look out across the cove to the ocean. There is a three-unit guest cottage and a separate cabin that sits—dramatically or precipitously, depending on one's point of view—at bluff's edge. Everywhere, there are flowers that seem casual, despite a gardener's care: "snow-in-season," felicia, California poppies, California wildflowers.

Van Damme State Park, Mendocino County, begins with sea stacks and driftwood and then offers inland trails and streams.

One spring evening, I asked to stay in the cabin on the edge. A memorable choice. It has two bedrooms, a long kitchen-dining-living-room space, a small balcony—all sloping gently seaward. The surf sweeps in below and the sounding buoy maintains its cadence of caution at the mouth of the river while gulls squeal in their passage to the green headland across the bay. Standing at the window, watching the wind kick up waves in the channel near the buoy, I had the feeling of being in a ship's cabin that was more or less firmly fixed to shore. Peter Wells, who runs the Albion River Inn with his wife Diana had told me that the cabin was built with wood from a shipwreck in the harbor and had given me a copy of the story of the incident: "The Wreck of the *Girlie Mahoney.*" The steamer, with a capacity of 400,000 feet of lumber, was set to sail for San Francisco just before Christmas 1919, when the stern line became entangled in the propeller. Efforts to free the line before darkness failed, and the next day, December 23, the seas became so rough that the crew could not control the ship. She struck the wharf, ripping off a section, and then was tossed aground on the beach. The crew was saved, but the *Girlie Mahoney* was pounded into wreckage.

I toasted the *Girlie Mahoney* and the crew's efforts to save her before walking down the path to dinner at the inn. There were a dozen seafood dishes on the menu, plus pasta, veal, duck and chicken entrees. I settled for the well-poached sole flamande, with mushrooms in wine. A dinner companion was equally enthusiastic about a large bowl of bouillabaisse with a salad. The featured wines are from nearby Anderson Valley and Mendocino wineries. After the sun is down beyond the Pacific horizon, the inn's lighting becomes a pleasant touch of evening. Appropriate light at dinner, particularly at a seaside setting, is as important as the right amount of tarragon on the breast of chicken. The Albion River Inn serves dinner daily from 5:30. For reservations, call 707-937-4044.

Peter Wells told me that the cabin I enjoyed may soon have to go the way of the ship that gave birth to it. There are plans to build another overnight unit on the near meadow. But he pointed out that the inn itself was partially supported by timber from the *Girlie Mahoney*.

Route 128 to Boonville is one of Mendocino County's major transverse roads and a most agreeable way to reach or depart from the coast. It branches off Highway 1 just below Albion and rolls through the lovely Anderson Valley to Boonville, where it connects with Route 253 to Ukiah; 128 continues to Cloverdale for a meeting with Highway 101. But the drive along the Navarro and Anderson Creek rewards with redwood stands, lush ranchlands and vineyards and leads to one of Mendocino's most famous restaurants, in Boonville.

About seven miles down the North Fork of the Navarro, Paul Dimmick Wayside Campground offers primitive campsites ($3) and a silent surrounding of redwoods. Near the town of Navarro, about 10 miles from the coast, the valley turns wide and green and is flowered with daffodils. I stopped late one morning at the Navarro Vineyards for a sampling of their Chardonnay Reserve. It tasted as good as it did from the dinner bottle at the Albion River Inn the night before. Like other Mendocino wineries, Navarro produces small lots; the 10,000 cases sold in a year include many direct sales to customers at the winery. Nearby on Highway 128, well-respected Husch Vineyards and Edmeades Vineyards have tasting rooms open daily to the public. Anderson Valley boasts "the most temperate climate in Mendocino," according to local folklore, and winegrowers have been attracted by the combination of ocean breeze and daily fog in the growing season.

To the west of the small town of Philo, **Hendy Woods State Park** covers 765 acres and offers fine walks through redwood groves on the flats of the Navarro River. Little Hendy and Big Hendy Grove to the south also have madrones, Douglas firs and California laurels, and in the open areas you will encounter deer fern, redwood sorrel and huckleberry. The picnic area at riverside has barbecue stoves. Two campgrounds have more than 80 sites.

Boonville is eight miles south on 128; the town also can be reached by the squirming, 24-mile Mountain View Road that meets Highway 1 just above Point Arena. For years, Boonville was known for its annual Apple Show and Fair at the Mendocino County Fairgrounds in early fall and for its vernacular known as "boontling." The town still celebrates its orchard crops, but boontling is not something you need to ask directions to the *New Boonville Hotel* which sits, as it has for years, on the edge of the wide main street. The vintage wooden hotel now attracts thousands of visitors who come to Boonville in all seasons to dine at the justifiably famous restaurant.

Owners Vernon and Charlene Rollins have developed a reputation for serving simple grilled meat and fish dishes thoughtfully enhanced with herbs from the garden behind the hotel, accompanied by salads and vegetables from their own produce. It is the only restaurant at which I eagerly eat the flowers that brighten the plate. A simple pizza lunch can be special when it is made with fennel root, red onion and smoked bacon; the sausage-in-pastry comes with pickled vegetables. The grilled chicken breast for dinner is stuffed with oregano, and the

mashed potatoes are made with chives and tarragon. A dinner
with wine will cost about $25; lunch can be moderate. The wine
list is exclusively Anderson Valley. No credit cards are accepted
and the menu indicates that a 15% service charge and 6% sales
tax are included in the prices. Reservations are necessary: 707–
895–3478. At lunchtime a stroll through the herb-vegetable-
flower gardens behind the clapboard inn is a fitting way to end
a visit to the New Boonville.

Mendocino

For a brief exploration of the forested interior of Mendocino, the
Flynn Creek Road, off 128 above Navarro, leads seven miles to
Comptche in timber country. Adventure in the interior can be
extended, if you are curious, by taking the sometimes-paved Orr
Springs Road that crosses the high ridge and follows the south
fork of the Big River as it descends toward Ukiah. It is 31 miles
of cautious driving, but it does pass the Montgomery Woods
State Reserve. For many years it was the only way, except for
the logging railroad, to go from the Mendocino-Fort Bragg
coastline to the Ukiah and Willits valleys. The distance from
Comptche to the coast—Little River or Mendocino Bay—is
about 14 miles.

Above Little River, **Van Damme State Park** runs inland
from a sandy beach into forest groves, covering nearly 350 acres.
A nature trail winds through the Pygmy Forest, with trees of
grotesquely stunted growth rooted in the hard soil. The Little
River is attractive fishing country. Campsites are available for
$6 overnight.

Even without its preserved, weathered, just-as-we-used-to-be
look, the town of **Mendocino** would have a character of its own,
if only because of its most eloquent location. The cliff-edged
promontory, surrounded by open sea and the Big River bay,
shapes the old lumbering center with its gently sloping streets.

The old-new face of the town of Mendocino brightens the bluffs above a small cove and a community beach.

Mendocino Headlands State Park protects the town's face to the sea and preserves the high bluffs and their giant wave tunnels and deep carvings for the townspeople and visitors to enjoy. There are blufftop trails to follow, ample parking and, at the mouth of the Big River, a small, sandy beach. Whenever I walk through town to the headlands, I envy the local residents who can take advantage of them in all weathers and seasons, particularly with spring calla lilies in bloom.

Mendocino's name was attached to the cape discovered by Juan Rodriguez Cabrillo in 1542 and chosen in honor of Don Antonio de Mendoza, first viceroy of New Spain. Approximately three hundred years later, Mendocino had its first sawmill and an economy that drew a racial mix of whites, Chinese and Portuguese. One of the latter, known as Portugee Frank, became a Mendocino legend by living in three centuries; he was born in 1797 and died in 1904. After their main store was burned to the ground, the Chinese settled in Fort Bragg, but the Portuguese maintained a lively presence in the community, segregating themselves in two rival areas as the Tar Flat Portuguese and the Fury Town—or East Mendocino—Portuguese. The groups originally came from the Azores to Hawaii, where they expected to work in the sugar fields. The need for jobs pulled them to the lumber towns of Northern California.

In the Mendocino Historical Society's oral history, John Fayal, born in Hawaii in 1888, recalled that for the Portuguese, the masquerade balls were the happiest form of entertainment. By playing the accordion, he received free drinks at parties, balls and in local saloons—plus change in the hat. A musician had wide choices. "There were 22 saloons in Mendocino at one time," he said. "I can count them: Needle's Saloon, Bill Groats's Saloon, Fernace Lemos's Saloon. Thomases' Saloon, Granskog's Saloon and Handelin's Saloon."

On his long list, Fayal mentioned **Mendosa's**, which still does business on Lansing Street—but in groceries and general merchandise. The **Mendocino Hotel** on Main Street opened for drinkers and overnight guests in 1878 and was modernized and expanded some 10 years ago. Next to the hotel, Dick's Place, where Bill Groats's once stood, holds the local record as the oldest saloon. **MacCallum House** (1882) on Albion Street bears an old Mendocino family name and a current strong reputation for its bar and restaurant. The **Ford House**, on the bay side of Main Street, was built in 1854, just after the start-up of the sawmill. The **Kelley House** (1861) is now a library and historical museum.

Mendocino's gin mills and sawmill are the abandoned part of a past that is preserved in an orderly and zealous manner by those who set the town's guidelines. Walk the streets—Mendocino is made for walking, for the gallery on Main near Highway 1 to the headlands—and the town's much-talked-of charm is displayed in its New England fishing village-style houses, with their unpainted picket fences, old wooden water towers and flowers bordered by driftwood. The Mendocino Historical Review Board has been charged with the responsibility of protecting the town against "Carmelization" (the building growth that engulfed Carmel, California). Its preservation ordinance, despite disputes, seems to have checked ostentatious development.

But it has not prevented a proliferation in the boutique busi-

The Mendocino Hotel, established in 1878, provided refuge for lumbermen and fishermen long before the tourists arrived.

ness that has spread from arcade to tiny frame shops with cutesy names, selling fashions, children's toys, antiques, pottery, ceramics, jewelry, local jellies, local flora, local art objects —all a tourist shopper on foot could hope to encounter.

Mendocino's colony of artists and artisans, which grows in size in the high season, has many gallery outlets in town. One does not have to be an art lover to appreciate the excellent **Mendocino Art Center and Gallery** on Little Lake. The center has an ambitious schedule of textile, ceramics, fine arts programs and frequently scheduled symposiums. (For example, the five-day workshop in basketry, held last year in late August, drew people long distances to learn the use of natural fibers, weaving, designing.) The center's juried art fairs, held at Thanksgiving and midsummer, show the works of local craftspeople. The regional exhibition space is occupied by works of California artists. The gallery, with over 180 artists-members, is open seven days a week throughout the year.

Mendocino has more than 20 hotels, bed & breakfast inns and cabin accommodations. Prices at the well-established lodges in the village itself are moderate to expensive. (**The Mendocino Hotel** and **Garden Houses** offer suites for $150 a night; double rooms at $85.) Several of the B & B's are appealing, period-furnished Victorian houses with ocean views. A complete listing for the area can be obtained from the Fort Bragg-Mendocino Coast Chamber of Commerce, PO Box 1141, Fort Bragg, California 95437 (Phone 707–964–3153). Houses in town are available for rent on a weekly or longer basis. Call Mendocino Coast Reservations 707–937–5033.

For dining choices, I have on two or three occasions turned to advice from locals who tend to eat out when the tourists have mostly gone. **The Seagull**, prominent on the corner of Ukiah and Lansing, is a popular choice for dependable food; it has a bustling cellarbar. **Brannan's Whale Watch Restaurant**, overlooking the bay, attracts tourists and local people who like to drink wine on the sun deck and watch the sea even when the whales are not expected on parade. **The Garden Cafe and Bar** at the Mendocino is a pleasant luncheon choice. **MacCallum's** historic lodge serves dinner only. Probably the best known, "most quaint" restaurant in Mendocino, **Cafe Beaujolais**, does a large breakfast and lunch business between 8:00 A.M. and 2:30 P.M. It has memorable omelettes—and a garden deck. Less well publicized is the **Wellspring Restaurant** next door and down the lane. It opens at 6:00 P.M. for dinners featuring vegetarian, seafood and stirfry chicken dishes. **The Chocolate Moosse**, a dessert cafe at the Blue Heron Inn, has day and evening hours. For the plain, hard hungry, the **Mendocino Ice Cream Factory**, a California fair medal winner, is the place to seek out on Main Street.

Russian Gulch State Park, on the north side of Mendocino off Highway 1, is another cove-and-forest area with 30 family campsites and 12 miles of inland and headland trails. The scenic bike trail extends for two and a half miles inland and the Falls Loop hiking trail reaches into the 53,000-acre Jackson State Forest. The creek canyon is covered with second-growth sequoia, Douglas fir, oak and California laurel. To the west of Highway 1, the cove has a picnic area, a small beach for day use, good skin diving and rock fishing possibilities. The high headland boasts a "blow-hole" some 100-feet across at the inland side of a tunnel cut by the sea. Waves rush through the tunnel, but the hole is too broad to provide much "blowing." Yet it is a spectacular headland to visit.

Jug Handle Creek crosses beneath Highway 1, five miles north of Mendocino, and a small state reserve affords another opportunity to observe the variations in tree growth resulting from an ecosystem development of a half-million years. On lower terraces near the sea, tree growth—cypress, pine, manzanita—appear normal. On the flat, higher terraces, the acidic hardpan soil has greatly reduced the size of trees. Some, perhaps a half-century old, stand only two- or three-feet tall. These pygmy forests are peculiar to the coast from Albion to Fort Bragg. Jug Handle Farm and Nature Center next to the reserve has private overnight accommodations.

Fort Bragg

The northbound traveler's introduction to Fort Bragg starts at the Noyo River, where the high bridge crosses the harbor, usually jammed with commercial fishing craft, charter boats, private pleasure cruisers. Fish-processing sheds, marine repair works, wholesale and retail markets and busy seafood restaurants compete for space in this protected fishing village. Fort Bragg and the neighboring Noyo harbor area have maintained the activities, to some degree, that have been the economic concerns for generations: fishing and lumbering. The latter industry in particular does shrink each year. It would take new building needs to bring back the boom years.

A fort did exist once at the townsite. Built inside the Mendocino Indian Reservation in the late 1850s, it was named for Mexican War general Braxton Bragg and served as a military post for nearly 10 years, until 1867, when the reservation was abandoned and the land was opened for settlement at less than

$2 an acre. As a fast-growing lumber center, Fort Bragg saw the Union Lumber Company develop a sawmill with a capacity of more than 300,000 feet a day. The lumberyards stretched long blocks near the rail yards west of Main Street. Now the Georgia-Pacific Corporation operates the "woods-products" division that is still a dominant feature of the city's business area. Residents and visitors alike are reminded of that by the plumes of smoke from tall stacks that are blown into high-riding remnants by ocean winds. The company's employment is down to approximately 1,000 (the Mendocino County government fills almost as many jobs). But the Mendo Mill Museum, open to the public near company headquarters on West Redwood Avenue, demonstrates what the lumber business once meant to Fort Bragg and the Northern California coast and how the harvesting of redwoods remains a highly visible part of the region's economy.

In his memories of Fort Bragg just after the turn of the century, Frank Hyman described what it was like to start young and at the bottom in lumbering. As a teenager he began making railroad ties, receiving 27¢ for a tie measuring 6 inches by 8 inches by 8 feet—for a total of $8.40 per thousand feet of wood. That also required swamping the ties—pulling them out of the forest to rugged roads by horse or sled—and then hauling them to the landing on the coast for shipment. Hyman said that the average tiemaker could produce about 20 ties a day.

I thought of Hyman's primitive lumbering experience as I watched the trailer rigs, with their chained loads of giant redwood logs, speeding by me on Highway 1 en route to modern mills.

From the Noyo River to Pudding Creek on the north edge of the city, Fort Bragg has a run of motels to choose from, most providing more economical overnight rates than do the inns of Mendocino. A prominent, reputable bed & breakfast lodge named **The Grey Whale** is located on North Main Street. However, I fell into the never-disappointing habit of staying at the **Surf**

An uneven fence and wildflowers are boundary enough for small Mendocino homes, which share the beauty of a grassy headland.

Motel, just across the Noyo River bridge on South Main Street. The owners describe their 50-odd units as "fastidiously clean," and they are well equipped and well removed from the busy highway. The motel has a small lending library in the office, a fish-cleaning facility is provided, and the "windshield caddy" dispenses towels hardy enough to remove the thick moisture that accumulates overnight from the sea across the road. Singles are $37; two-room kitchenettes are available (Phone: 707-964-5361). For a detailed listing of motels and inns in the Fort Bragg area, call the Chamber of Commerce (707-964-3153) or visit the center at 332 North Main Street.

The **Noyo Harbor**, which has a lengthy mooring basin on the south side, is most easily reached by North Harbor Drive off Highway 1. The harbor is worth visiting for a meal, a fish purchase, a boat charter or simply a long look at the passing parade of vessels. Arrive early, around 7:00 A.M., and you can see the 44-foot *Lady Irma II or Trek II* on their daily charter runs for salmon or for bottom fish, such as ling cod, red snapper, rock cod. Cap'n Flint's Restaurant and The Wharf Restaurant and Lounge do a heavy lunch and dinner business at dockside. If you're in the market for used netting or a carton of fish chowder to go, they are easy to find at the fishing village.

The Noyo River, its north fork flanked by the Skunk Railroad tracks, runs a long distance from the interior and is a productive steelhead stream. On one January visit to Fort Bragg, I heard about the local fisherman who had taken the lead in the annual December through March steelhead derby with a catch of 20 pounds. I was told that the river was unusually low and clear, which encouraged fishermen to spread out more. Salmon roe and silver flatfish were recommended bait.

My first choice for serious dining in the Fort Bragg vicinity is **Casa del Noyo,** which combines an appealing harbor ambience and good cuisine. It is a small Victorian inn set among cypress trees above the boat basin, rustic and comfortable enough for most tastes. The redwood bar with fireplace is the proper first stop on a late fall or winter evening; a window table for dinner is a wise reservation request. Even without an easy view of the rigging lights and cabin glow of the fishing boats, a table at Casa del Noyo is made comfortable by candlelight and a carafe of the Mendocino house wine. The menu includes a quail entree at $15.95 and dependable ling cod at half that price. The dinner salads are excellent. The inn has six well-furnished guestrooms, with a buffet or room-service breakfast (Phone: 707–964–5354). It's located on Casa del Noyo Drive at the north side of the harbor.

The Fort Bragg Chamber of Commerce, the Georgia Pacific Logging Museum (and a tour of the mill) and the California Western Railroad headquarters for the "Skunk" trains are all within a short walking distance between Laurel and Oak Avenues on or just off North Main. For the summer and reduced winter schedule of daily trains departing from Fort Bragg, call 707–964–6371 or write California Western Railroad, PO Box 907, Fort Bragg, California 95437. (For background on the "Skunk" trains and how they grew, see pp. 139–140.)

The local Chamber of Commerce promotes a busy calendar of events along the upper Mendocino coast; no matter when you visit, there seems to be a festival, a feed, a concert or a celebration in progress. Fort Bragg is proud of its Fourth of July parade, which the town has held for generations, during which time it produces "the world's largest salmon barbecue." Whales and whale-watching get a lot of attention in March. The Fort Bragg orchid show and the Whale Festival arrive, stem to sperm, during the last week of the month. Prime whale-watching periods are January through March, although November and December offer opportunities up and down the California coast.

Whale-Watching

I don't know why I have such a shoddy whale-watching record. I have considered possible reasons: bad timing, poor eyesight, fogged binoculars, lack of concentration, susceptibility to seagoing mirages, headland distractions. It could be one or several of those factors that contribute to my embarrassing inability to speak of happy whale sightings. I have been tempted to conclude that all those people who crowd the shoreline from Point Reyes and beyond are looking for whales and seeing sea lions, as I invariably do, and that those who pay dearly for seats on whale-tracking seaplanes or for space on whale-following charter boats don't dare admit the failure I encounter from blufftop and sandy sea level.

It is estimated that more than 15,000 California gray whales now migrate from Arctic feeding grounds to the breeding waters off Baja California each winter and that they follow a predictable, near-shore cruise course. Since they travel about four or five knots an hour and the most mature of them reach over 40 feet in length, the chances of spotting one or several would seem high. I have been told that if you are disappointed by the performance of whales off Point Arena, Gualala or Bodega Bay, you can take the short trip from San Francisco to the lighthouse in the Point Reyes National Seashore to see their gala act of appreciation for being saved from extinction. (The grays are still protected under international treaty; Alaskan Eskimos can take but 10 each year, the Soviet Union is restricted to 179 kills.)

One late February morning, I hurried out to Manchester Beach after reading in the *Independent Coast Observer* that a young woman named Debbie from Anchor Bay had been given a personal performance at the beach by a huge southbound whale. It breached 10 times and Debbie began to cheer above the crashing surf, apparently delighting the whale, which twice flashed its flukes as it plowed beneath the surface. But from my perch atop a heavy driftwood log, I searched the rising and falling sea without success. Lovely, dark blue and streaked with whites and grays—but only the ocean.

I talked to a park ranger about my problem. He suggested that if I was heading north I should try the Point Arena Light. "Bar none," he said, "it is the best place to whale-watch in Northern California." I refrained from telling him that I had already done considerable time at the top of the lighthouse without improving my record. Earlier, I had talked to a whale-watcher at Bodega Harbor who had taken the whale run on the 65-foot *Mary Jane* ($20 per person) and had been treated to a skyhopping performance by a huge gray. Skyhopping—thrusting the head well above the waves—is apparently a whale's way of counting the house—on shore or aboard spectator craft. He told me I should call the Whale-Watch Phone (415-474-3385), manned by the Oceanic Society in San Francisco, for guidance and also for the schedule of whale-watching expeditions that depart regularly during the season from Pillar Point in Princeton-by-the-Sea, San Mateo County.

But I was determined to score on my own, somewhere between Bodega Bay and Eureka, even in face of the threat of becoming an endangered species myself: a whale-watcher without a sighted whale.

Leave the city limits of Fort Bragg, northbound on Highway 1, and you are quickly invited by road sign to explore **MacKerricher State Park**, which encompasses a long sandy beach, a six-mile equestrian trail, picnic sections, a 143-unit camping area and small Lake Cleone with freshwater fishing. Walk to the headland at Laguna Point and there is a good chance of seeing a show of harbor seals who frequent area waters. Within the park area, an unusual hiking-biking route closely follows the coast for a half-dozen miles. It is identified as the Georgia-Pacific Haul Road and has been long used by logging trucks as a Highway 1 bypass. Recently, severe storm damage closed the road but repairs were expected to return it to hauling use. It remains open to the public on weekends, a wide, welcome beach-side path for walkers, joggers, cyclists.

The highway swerves inland at Cleone, hurrying through stands of pine and cypress until it crosses Ten Mile River and then picks up its seaside course again. Undeveloped beaches and blufftop viewing spaces occupy much of the way to the town of Westport. The stretch is ideal for parking and then finding the thin walking trail through waving grass to the headland for a view or for the access that leads down to rock fishing possibilities.

Westport

When I think of Westport, I think of horses standing patiently at meadow fences, small houses that seem to have been scattered at random across the sloping shoreline, a wonderful seascape—and little to suggest that a busy port once existed here. The town's name was provided by an early resident who came from Eastport, Maine. In the late 1800s, there were two large wharves and unending tanbark cords awaiting shipment. In 1881, it was predicted that Westport "will be one of the liveliest towns on the coast," since it had already acquired three hotels, six saloons, two blacksmith shops, three stores and two livery stables. On December 3, 1881, a message from Westport, as recorded in the *Mendocino Historical Review,* said that the shipping season had ended with 50 schooners calling at the port

Once a thriving mill town and shipping center, Westport is now a small residential community with a splendid seascape all its own.

since April. Tanbark cords for downstate tanneries, shakes, posts and firewood from several nearby mills—there was a large one at Rockport just up the coast and another on the Hollow Tree Road—were shipped out, and freight bound for the inland was unloaded. A 375-foot wharf was equipped with wooden chutes; later, cable chutes speeded the loading process.

Westport was then compared with Mendocino in shipping importance and as a favored coast town with trim, painted houses and a lively commercial and barroom environment. It was sheltered by Cape Mendocino to the far north and the high rise of hills to the east. Viewed from the sea, however, the rocky, uneven coast had a forbidding appearance, and ships' crews were advised to "give the lee shore a wide berth."

In the summer of 1883, it was noted that "the stages are performing the extraordinary feat of leaving Ukiah at sunrise and setting down passengers in Westport before sunset the next day." So it was possible for a traveler to leave San Francisco, spend an overnight in Ukiah, and arrive in Westport the following morning. (Today's coastal highway route is over 200 miles.)

Burt Chapman, a minister's son, grew up in Westport in the early 1900s, and in *Mendocino County Remembered* he recalls that the town was "a beautiful place to live. Of course I didn't know any different but my folks enjoyed it. . . . The church in Westport was right next to the parsonage. We were about 50 feet from the bluff. Out our kitchen window was the garden and then a steep drop. . . . The cemetery was out there just north of town. Wage's Creek—my father used to baptise right in the creek; it was a big Sunday affair."

Westport's prosperous days did not stretch far into the new century. By the end of World War I, it was assuming the look of a ghost town. The last mill closed in 1920, and the Fort Bragg to Willits rail link took freight business away from Westport. But a visit to the village today suggests some of the charm that Burt Chapman felt as a young boy. Along the short, ocean-front street are a half-dozen houses, some recently refurbished, facing the restless surf. Turn off the highway on Omega Drive, then up Abalone to Seaview, down Seaview past the Cobweb Palace, and you have seen much of the immediate town.

Built of redwood in the 1890s, **The Cobweb Palace** is the only remnant of a dozen or more hotels that once served the town. It has seven bed & breakfast rooms, a short but appealing dinner menu, and a cramped, old-inn feeling about it that is particularly attractive on a late fall evening. Prices are moderate, and the sunset glow in front of the inn can be stunning. (Phone: 707–964–5588). An art gallery is comfortably located next door. There are two recommended bed & breakfast ranches just north of Westport: The **Dehaven Valley Farm** (Phone: 707–964–2931) and the **Howard Creek Ranch** (Phone: 707–964–6725). The latter was developed by Frank Howard in a pleasant east-west valley in the 1870s. The **Westport Inn**, a small motel, is located in the village on Highway 1 and is connected to the **Westport Deli** just behind a picket fence. It is a choice roadside stop for breakfast or lunch, indoors or out. A "Branscomb Charlie" sandwich to go—avocado, cheese, egg salad, tomato, sprouts on dark rye—will last you many miles, north or south.

Westport-Union Landing State Beach is a lengthy day-use area, with access to the beach below, a little north of town. It and the overlooks beyond are good locations to view the ocean before making the steep inland climb that Highway 1 takes outside Rockport. The coastline mostly drops from view after you pass Juan Creek Beach and the warning road sign: "Narrow Winding Road Next 22 Miles/Watch Out for Bicycles." The narrow, ill-surfaced Usal Road does continue up the Mendocino Coast toward the **Sinkyone Wilderness State Park**. But this undeveloped parkland is much better approached from the north via Garberville and Shelter Cove. (See next chapter.)

Continue on Highway 1, which was/is the old Hollow Tree logging road, and you face a driving challenge, despite the many caution signs and the good, hard surface. At every sharp twist you should anticipate meeting an oncoming trailer truck heavily burdened with logs. If you are steering a compact, it is hard to escape the occasional fear that you will get squashed by rolling logs or shunted off the trail and into the valley far below. It is a good test of driving skills—and your courage, if you have not recently placed it on a swerving line.

This high ridge is Louisiana-Pacific territory, and the ugly sight of clear-cutting, the whine from saws and portable mills, the grinding of truck and heavy-equipment gears, become part of the journey. It is difficult here to believe that the timber business is in decline, that most of the production now comes from company land, the Mendocino National Forest, and not from private holdings. Redwood is the most harvested of Northern California softwoods; less Douglas fir is going to market. The timber boom peaked around 1960, but the redwood remains a valuable commodity. It is fast growing, rejuvenates well and is resistant to disease and fire. More than a million and a half acres of redwood forest are located within a belt along the Northern California coast that extends some 40 miles inland. This is where the increasingly intense battle between environmentalists and timber-products people has been fought.

To Leggett

I find it useful to break the long run between the coast and
Leggett, or vice versa, by stopping at one of the many turnouts
and taking a walk. You may look down on distant, red-brown
logging roads or a patch of white birches at creekside or a
sudden green pasture with grazing cattle. At Hales Grove you
will find a table factory to check out, and there is always an
assortment of redwood burl for sale. I have happily escaped bad
weather on this road stretch—but I am usually relieved to see
the sea westbound or to come into the flat valley outside Leggett
when I drive from the coast. Highway 1 and a divided section of
north-south 101 meet outside this small community. Leggett
promotes a "Drive-Thru Tree" ($2) with an adjacent "Relaxa-
tion Area." On the main street you will note a small diner, the
"World Famous Leggett Market" (very well stocked), the Leggett Motel ("country cabins" at economical rates), service stations. It is a comfortable jumping-off place if you are heading
north into redwood territory or turning south on 101 to Laytonville and the Willits and Ukiah valleys.

Laytonville, a swift valley run of 20-plus miles from Leggett,
is also reachable from Westport and the coast by the old Branscomb Road, which follows DeHaven Creek into the ridge. However, it is not a wide, easy lateral route. A dozen miles east of
Laytonville, the Northwestern Pacific Railroad tracks cross the
road at Dos Rios, and you can follow them south through open
country toward Willits or head north to Covelo at the edge of
the Round Valley Indian Reservation, one of the largest in the
state.

Round Valley was open range country in the late 1800s, the
domain of influential ranchers like George White who ran huge
herds of cattle and sheep and discouraged homesteaders from
occupying the land. For years, Indians and whites ran their
cattle together on favored reservation grasslands where Indians
lived in brush-hut settlements. The high ridges that cut through

the reservation reach over 4,000 feet; the valleys are rich in feed grass.

Above Leggett, the south fork of the Eel River dictates the traffic route through the northwest corner of Mendocino County. The road twists and turns with the river canyon, and there are dramatic views of its course if you manage to make the right stop. One late spring day, I backed into an abandoned portion of the original 101 and then walked it for a distance, picking wildflowers and looking down at the Eel. A dominating and fascinating river, its branches cut through much of this part of Northern California. The Eel and the redwoods provide one of the most majestic matchups you will find in any river valley.

There are two nearly adjacent forest preserves on 101, a short distance from Leggett: the Standish-Hickey State Recreation Area and the Smithe/Redwoods State Reserve. The former has family camping facilities and the reserve, three miles north, is fine for a picnic or a walk. As 101 approaches the county line it acquires a commercial-tourist look, with signs leading to the "Believe It or Not Tree House" or the "Log O' Legends," dedi-

Fast flows the Eel—a river whose branches bring life and sport to the region —through a southern Humboldt County canyon.

cated to "Truckerman Josh." Less-than-legendary Louisiana-Pacific truckers now pull their rigs up to favorite fast-food and diesel fuel stops scattered along the route. The impressive sequoia groves and peaceful state parks are but a short drive north.

HUMBOLDT COUNTY

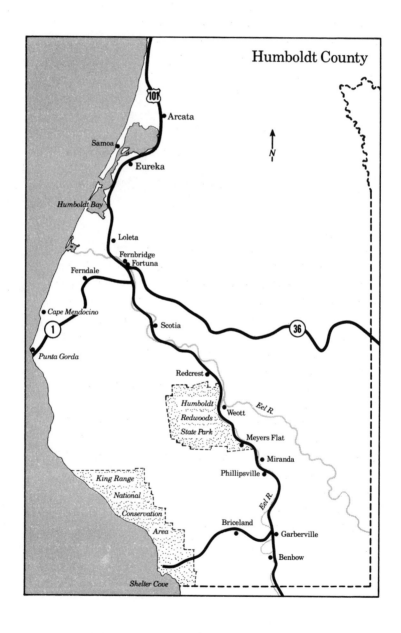

I T is significant that Humboldt County introduces itself with dark stillness mixed with slivers of sunlight in **Richardson Grove State Park**, a great towering of redwoods *(Sequoia sempervirens)* along the Eel River basin on Route 101. Humboldt is visited redwood country on the coastal side; to the east are creeks, rivers, forests, mountains and long distances of light and darkness between places where people live. Richardson is a prime example of the state park system's ability to offer environmental grandeur and a variety of well-maintained facilities within a confined space: easy walking paths and a picnic zone in the redwood groves; family camping (169 sites in three areas); river swimming in the summer; winter fishing for salmon and steelhead; a few ambitious loop trails for hikers. The park office near the highway can provide a map and information (for camping reservations, call 707–247–3318). Yet by making only a brief stop you can appreciate what hundreds of years of soil deposits from the Eel have accomplished: remarkable coniferous trees that grow straight to taller-than-steeple heights.

Benbow

Beyond the park limits, approaching Benbow State Recreation Area, I look for Benbow Drive, which puts me in close touch with the Eel again. In the spring and late season, the waters are swift and brilliantly green, and the wind can be noisy as it pushes through the trees. If you are lucky, you may see a fish hawk—the osprey—far above, riding the wind, then banking down to check the river below. You hope that it will be encouraged to descend and strike the water, but even in its high-altitude surveillance, it is a dramatic fisherman.

Tall and Tudor-styled, the Benbow Inn has been welcoming guests to its lofty rooms outside Garberville since 1926.

The river road is my way of reaching the **Benbow Inn**, highly visible on its hillside, whichever direction you are heading on 101. It is one of the few landmark inns that deserves its place on the map and in updated lists of recommended lodgings. Opened to the public in 1926, it has had an impressive—if not unbroken —history of endorsement. The partially timbered, Tudor-style inn stands brightly above a bow in the south fork of the Eel, but the name comes from the family who originally selected this unusual hotel site and had it built. In the warm season, a one-mile lake is formed just below the inn by holding the waters of the east branch of the Eel where it joins the south fork. The small swimming and boating water is part of the Benbow Lake State Recreation Area, which has developed sites for campers and day-users.

The first time I checked into the Benbow, on a late April afternoon, the woman at the desk greeted me as if she had personally anticipated my arrival. "We serve tea and scones in the lobby at four," she said. "The bar opens at four-thirty. And, oh, yes, our movie tonight is *The Little Foxes* with Bette Davis!" The third-floor room (as high as you can go) overlooking the terrace and flower beds was furnished with the heavy furniture that invites you to stay. The floor squeaked quietly. On the bureau, a decanter of port stood next to a basket of books, most of them mysteries. I decided to begin rereading John Buchan's *The Thirty-Nine Steps* before taking tea in the lobby.

The lobby demands exploration. It is a successful mélange of Victorian chairs, several tall case clocks that don't strike, old family portraits, bronze figures, ivory figures, a carousel horse, almost-but-not-quite finished jigsaw puzzles on small tables. I thumbed through the Benbow scrapbook and learned that Charles Laughton memorized the lines for *Mutiny on the Bounty* while staying at the inn. Among the many famous guests of the past were Eleanor Roosevelt and Herbert Hoover. A 1945 luncheon menu offered "Little Pig Sausage en Surprise" and "Pounded Luncheon Steak Old Style."

The inn's many-windowed dining room has a capacity of 140, but guests are advised to reserve a seating well ahead. The menu is strong on French and seafood dishes and makes admirable use of fresh vegetables. At dinner's end, my Tudor-frocked waitress, Linda, suggested that I might wish to take my wine to the lobby. I finished it while viewing the passing parade from an unupholstered settee. The bar off the lobby, with a large fireplace working on cool nights and a terrace open in seasonable weather, is a pleasant common room in which to begin or end an evening. Rooms in the original building are $62 to $95. The new, larger terrace rooms are $95 to $125. The inn has special second-night rates during the off-season. Reservations for holiday periods should be made far in advance (Phone: 707–923–2124).

Garberville

Garberville, the near town, is three miles from the Benbow Inn, and it sits strategically above the south fork of the Eel. It was named for John C. Garber, who settled in the area because he saw a future for stock-raising. He probably could not have foreseen the ups and downs in agriculture and lumber, the arrival and departure of the railroad. Nor would he have imagined the community's growing attraction for tourists, who may choose to take advantage of the recreation offered by the Eel, the redwood forests and the coastal range. In the last several years, Garberville also acquired an unwonted reputation as a hub of marijuana trade. Northern California's largest, and certainly most famous, cash crop has centered in the Emerald Triangle (Mendocino, Humboldt and Del Norte counties), and the town has found itself prominent in headlines about the conflict between growers and increasingly aggressive law enforcers.

The town does not immediately suggest that it is a mini Las Vegas, ringing with profits that originate in clandestine sites in nearby woods and hills. It seems to be a one-street town with a line of motels, a scattering of shops and moderate eating places and a weekly newspaper, the *Redwood Record*, which celebrated its fiftieth publishing anniversary in 1985.

Long before its identification with outlaw agriculture, Garberville was known to northwest fishermen working the Eel and its tributaries in southern Humboldt. As a sportsman's center, it takes civic pride in a fish-development program conducted by local volunteers with the cooperation of the California Conservation Corps. Nearby rearing ponds have produced approximately 40,000 steelhead and 10,000 king salmon in a season. It is possible to visit one of the creek sites by inquiring at the tourist information booth in Garberville or by checking with the Rotary Club, a program sponsor.

On the broad river flat below the business area, Garberville has created a small park that runs handsomely through redwoods and glades. Tooby Park was dedicated in 1967 to the memory of three Tooby brothers—Frank, Ernest and Ira—and even the one-time visitor to the town should seek it out, no matter what the season. Stop early at the Eel River Cafe on Redwood Drive, Garberville's main street, pick up coffee and a breakfast roll and take it down to Tooby Park to watch the mist lift slowly from the river and redwood stands.

Shelter Cove

One morning, as a blue sky slowly revealed itself above the river, I decided to make my first trip over the **King Range** to Shelter Cove on the ocean at the southern tip of Humboldt. At Redway, Garberville's adjoining town, turn left at the Shelter Cove Grotto, a bar and restaurant, and follow the signs to Briceland and beyond. It is 23 miles on a well-paved, serpentine road to Shelter Cove.

The King Range rises moderately from the interior and plunges precipitously toward the sea. The summit of Kings Peak reaches 4,087 feet from sea level in less than three miles. This is rugged, mostly undeveloped coast country, with 54,000 acres designated as a National Conservation Area under the Bureau of Land Management. It covers 30 miles along the coast and about six miles inland, from the mouth of the Mattole (a recreation site above Punta Gorda) to Point No Pass in Mendocino County. There it connects with the **Sinkyone Wilderness State Park**, a coastal reserve of 3,600 undeveloped acres. This park can be reached from Bear Harbor on the Usal Road that connects with the Briceland Road.

Although there are sections, particularly around Shelter Cove, that are privately held, most of this wild, spectacular conservation area is open to the public for hiking, hunting and fishing. Four recreation sites in the southern end are equipped for camping. There are trails of varying difficulty throughout the mountain range. The 16-mile King Crest Trail follows the ridge above Shelter Cove and takes you as high as you need be above the empty coastline for a wilderness perspective. From Kings Peak, one can look down on Rattlesnake Ridge and Big Flat Creek, which drop hurriedly to the sea. It is possible to walk the beach from the Mattole River to Shelter Cove, about 24 miles, although it is wise to check tide charts when planning the journey. Hikers are advised to carry sufficient drinking water.

A basic map and guide for the King Range can be obtained from the District Manager, U.S. Bureau of Land Management, 555 Leslie Street, Ukiah 95482. Guides and information are also available in Shelter Cove.

Weaving down the ridge into Shelter Cove, one is immediately struck by the network of newly paved roads leading to recently built homes or, more vividly, to empty lots. The familiar design of a development spreads across slopes above the cove —a subdivision of more than 4,000 lots. Because of this real estate venture, the route over the King Range has changed from an upgraded logging road to a highway. And Shelter Cove has taken another turn in its history: from an abandoned fishing and shipping port on California's "Lost Coast" to a recreation and retirement community building on its scenic location.

Shelter Cove went through boom and bust periods similar to those experienced at many coastal points, but its location on the far side of the King Range slowed its rediscovery and recovery. Indian tribes—the Whilkut, Sinkyone and Mattole—who occupied the area before the arrival of whites apparently used the cove and beaches as seasonal resources. But it wasn't until early settlers saw the advantage of establishing a shipping center

In developing Shelter Cove, once a place name on the Lost Coast, a seafood restaurant makes a modern point toward the sea.

here for tanoak and tanbark extract in the 1880s that it took on the form of a community. When the tanoak demand fell, Shelter Cove became a depot for fish processing, an industry in which the Machi, Alioto and Lazio families were locally prominent. Shelter Cove's small facilities and its lack of dependable access narrowed its possibilities as a commercial port. In the mid-1930s it had become a place name on the "Lost Coast."

Shelter Cove's reputation as a resort and retirement area grows by slow degrees. If you visit after the rainy season in the King Range (late fall and winter) and before May 1 you will find a couple of stores open and the two main restaurants on weekend schedules. The marine and fishing supply outlets are in business, the sea can be viewed and reached from many angles and the county airport, with its lengthy beach strip, is open when weather permits. Although still remote and shielded from the inland by that towering range, Shelter Cove now sees year-round traffic flow.

On a return from Shelter Cove one late spring day, I stopped near the summit and, with lunch and field glasses in a canvas bag, took off on a trailless hike. I had passed the road leading to the Tolkan and Horse Mountain camping areas and, according to the map, was heading in the general direction of Queen Peak. The day was strong with sun and a wind that seemed to be scraping relentlessly at the top of the world. Lupine was everywhere, adding its patches of blue to the mountain floor. I walked on, looking for the ideal stopping place on this ridge above the Pacific.

I noticed a helicopter moving slowly over the coastline—on a beach watch, I supposed. But I didn't hear it until it swung inland over the ridge and headed in my direction. The beat of the engine came and went in the high wind, but the helicopter thrust toward me, as if cued by a film script. It lowered and circled twice and then flew north along the ridge. As I walked I felt a rising sense of being intimidated on this solo hike on a sparkling day in the King Range. When, in short minutes, the helicopter returned and banked even closer I put down the clutch of lupine I had picked and reached for my field glasses. It wasn't until I tried to focus on the hard-thumping machine that I realized I was under some sort of surveillance, most likely a CAMP (Campaign Against Marijuana Planting) flyover checking public lands. I was a possible grower out to see how my garden was faring. I retrieved my bouquet of alpine flowers and waved them vigorously at the crew of the helicopter. It did the trick. The helicopter turned, picked up speed and flew off in search of greener patches.

Back in Garberville, I learned that CAMP, which consists of local and state agencies and county sheriffs' offices, had begun its surveillance of public lands with helicopter and fixed-wing teams that would lead to eradication raids in July. I was asked if I thought that the searching helicopter had remained 500 feet above ground. It was too noisy for measurement, I said. Because of complaints by residents of obtrusive practices by CAMP, flying restrictions had been set by local courts—and then challenged by federal authorities.

If marijuana cultivation has become the surprising replacement of lumbering as a private enterprise in the backcountry along the Northern California coast, it has produced effects similar to those of the booze trade during Prohibition. Local, law-abiding citizens, who received secondhand profit from bootleggers, were inclined to tolerate the illegal practice as long as it did not interfere with their private lives. In an issue devoted to marijuana's impact on the region, the *Ridge Review,* an enterprising quarterly published in Mendocino, reported that "most shop and store owners along the Coastal Ridges, as well as many skilled and unskilled laborers, realize some indirect income from marijuana. Many of them know it and so cater to the grower through advertising, choice of merchandise, or by simply being discreet. Some marijuana money reaches the pockets of at least 40% of the population by indirect means."

Drive from Garberville to Briceland or take the hilly back-

road east to Alderpoint, on a large Eel River bend, and you get
some feel for the land that has, through changing times, thinly
sustained homesteaders, farmers, loggers, sawmill workers,
moonshiners, retirees, urban dropouts and back-to-nature converts. Some of these new emigrés became small-scale marijuana
cultivators whose profits enabled them to maintain a lifestyle
based heavily on self-sufficiency.

In *Cash Crop: An American Dream,* author Ray Raphael, a
resident and a careful observer of this coastal countryside, comments: "History has a way of defying our normal expectations.
No unemployed logger in 1965 could possibly have guessed that
an illegal weed that takes six months to grow would fetch a
higher price than a thousand-year-old tree. . . . In the mid-1970s
the new pioneers were on the verge of developing a cash crop
that would flourish beyond their wildest fantasies. [But] the
marijuana industry would prove to be both the joy and sorrow
of the idealistic movement that fostered it. It would push the
rebels still further out on the edges, yet it would also trigger a
peculiar sort of re-entry into the mainstream society they once
had so thoroughly rejected."

Raphael's reasoned examination of the marijuana boom is
presented largely in first-person accounts from people effected
by the industry: among them, a single mother and small-time
grower, a marijuana trimmer in a large operation, a high school
principal, the former head of the Garberville-Redway Chamber
of Commerce, the deputy commander of CAMP. The spectrum
of views provides an education on the subject for the outsider
and also a revealing look at the rural society of this part of
Northern California. Raphael chose his witnesses well.

I was not on hand in the Garberville area for the big July 1985
bust that CAMP and federal officials said helped reduce the crop
by 40%. The paramilitary operation was monitored by the Citizens Observation Group, formed to report violations of helicopter flight ceilings and harassment of residents on the ground.
There were local cheers and local complaints concerning the

crackdown—and, of course, doubts about CAMP's claims of success. The annual marijuana crop cannot be measured as accurately as soybeans. If growers were indeed sent fleeing to more distant hills, the exodus would eventually be reflected in the economy, one that has seen ups and downs in local agriculture before.

Redwoods

It can be argued that redwood country starts south of San Francisco in the Big Sur or just north of the city in Muir Woods, and that the Redwood Highway (101) runs close to enough groves to satisfy any sequoiaphile. Yet it can also be said that until you have reached the **Avenue of the Giants** in Humboldt County, a section of the old, two-lane 101, you have not really entered the forest and encountered the trees. The avenue, probably the most famous redwood route in the world, runs 33 miles along the south fork of the Eel and through the 51,000-acre **Humboldt Redwoods State Park**. Its size and accessibility make it the choicest of redwood preserves, although the Prairie Creek and Jediah Smith stands in the larger Redwood National Park at the top of the county are both impressively primeval. (The national park also boasts the world's tallest tree—367-plus feet.)

The southern access to the Avenue of the Giants above Garberville is well marked at the Redwood Burl Factory. The road, paralleled by the fast lanes of 101, leads to Phillipsville, which is the first of a half-dozen small towns along the way that thrive, as best they can, by selling wood products, provisions and meals to tourists and by providing motel accommodations to those who prefer to camp close to a TV and a heated swimming pool. Past Phillipsville you encounter the first designated grove and picnic area, the Franklin K. Lane Grove, located at a sharp bend in the Eel and favored at the west end by Fish Creek.

The road runs close to the Eel until the town of Miranda,

which offers overnight cottages and a sizable market; it then cuts into parkland again. At Dry Creek, a sign directs to a horse trail, one of some 100 miles of hiking and riding trails that lace this redwoods park. They vary in length from a half mile to seven-plus miles; some are only a stroll, but a few are arduous climbs. Hikers who want to make the round-trip from park headquarters to the lookout at Grasshopper Peak, which rises 3,379 feet in the center of the park, are advised to allow about eight hours—and to let someone at the ranger office know that they are starting the journey. (Park headquarters and the visitor center are located approximately at the halfway point on the Avenue of the Giants; they are just south of Weott.)

In addition to the trails, groves, picnic areas and campgrounds (three, with a total of 247 campsites), the park has a half-dozen trail camps with piped water. The Whiskey Flat Trail Camp, which can be approached by taking the Bull Creek Flats Road north of park headquarters, got its name from an old Prohibition still that was hidden there. It is at the edge of the Rockefeller Forest, pleasantly guarded by mature redwoods. The nearby Hansom Ridge Trail Camp is superbly located on heights above Bull Creek. Most trail camps are available on a first-come-first-served basis. Reservations are required for family and group campgrounds and also for environmental campsites. Any visitor who plans to spend a day or longer in the forests should be equipped with a Humboldt Redwoods State Park brochure and map, obtainable at park headquarters or by writing to PO Box 100, Weott 95571. (Phone: 707–946–2311.)

If you have no overnight camping or ambitious trail walking in mind and are content with driving the avenue and making a stop or two, there are groves to choose beyond the exit to the town of Myers Flat (another Drive-Thru tree, gift shops, a motel and a recommended coffee shop called Dave's). For example, the Garden Club of America Grove (standard $2 day-use fee) has a mile-and-a-quarter trail that connects with those leading through the Williams Grove area and then across the river to

The Avenue of the Giants in Humboldt County winds through redwood forests, which command the respect of every traveler.

the Hidden Springs campground. The Founders Grove—site of the park's tallest tree—is dedicated to those who started the Save-the-Redwoods League in 1918; it has a short nature trail with informative markers.

There are about 100 memorial groves in the park, the result of the league's long preservation efforts. I have a favorite, not far off the main road, which I have found pleasantly deserted even though an old access to a broad sweep of the Eel is close by. It is located near the 23-mile marker as you approach Redcrest on Humboldt 254. The grove is not indicated on most maps, but near the small parking area above the river, resting among low ferns, is the stone identification marker: "In Memory of Andy Bowman/Mendocino County Pioneer."

It is a small grove with redwoods of no record height, but their proximity to the river and their reach into the sky give the place a certain majesty. My discovery of the grove was made the more memorable by the spread of spring wildflower blooms—trillium and the five-petal redwood sorrel, a generous gift of lavender to the pattern of colors on the forest floor. If the redwoods stand so close and tall that the sun is allowed to reach the ground only in spotlight bursts, these magnificent trees do permit ferns and flowers lavish display room. Their thick-ribbed, cinnamon colored trunks are free of branches for nearly one third of their height, which, even in these dense groves, may reach over 300 feet. The coast redwood—*Sequoia sempervirens:* "ever-living" because of its regenerative strength—is not as old or as thick as the Sierra Nevada variety. But it reaches greater heights and may date back 1,500 years or more.

The coast redwoods need the fog of summer and rain of winter to thrive, but I encountered only sunshine on my visits to Andy Bowman Grove. One day, I picked a sorrel and stuck it between my teeth as I had seen school children in Redcrest do. It has a vaguely bitter, not unpleasant taste, and I reminded myself to use a stem or two in my luncheon salad. Walking the loop trail, I wondered how these famous trees came to bear the name of the Indian scholar Sequoya, whose influence was with the Cherokees, one of the Five Civilized Tribes, its members forcibly removed from the southeast to Oklahoma reservations. Sequoya created a table of syllables for the tribe's language, and on this day there was, I decided, something linguistic about the redwood grove I walked through. A steady wind tossed the branches with their pine needles and cones far above me, a loud, unthreatening sound that I had seldom heard. I wondered if perhaps some of these trees near the narrow trail were longtime survivors of past redwood slaughter and had been speaking the same wind words during the time of the Crusades, Genghis Khan and Charlemagne before him! My romantic speculation was interrupted by the distant, modern warning whistle of a diesel engine. I walked toward the river and climbed a huge redwood log for a look. The Eel split into two channels here, forming a sandbar in the middle, and the wind whipped puffs of sand into the air. On the opposite bank was a lengthy break in the redwoods and I could see the stretch of rail. Soon a Northwestern Pacific freight came into view, moving slowly north. It occurred to me that the train crew was working a rare, scenic run, viewing the Humboldt redwoods for so many miles as a green backdrop to the wide riverbed. Surrounded by trees dedicated to Andy Bowman, I was sure I had the best of both worlds.

Scotia, Fortuna, Fernbridge and Ferndale

The long redwood belt extends northward beyond the park limits, but the Avenue of Giants access comes near Pepperwood, about six miles beyond Redcrest. From Pepperwood it is approximately 30 miles on 101 to Eureka.

The redwoods as a commodity are on view as you approach the town of **Scotia**, named for Nova Scotia because so many early settlers and lumbermen came from there. Scotia is one of the last company towns in Northern California. (Samoa, across Humboldt Bay from Eureka, is another.) Pacific Lumber, the parent company, has been in business here since 1886. Great stacks of lumber and logs dominate the landscape, and although the mill, occupying about 400 acres, does not provide the variety of wood products it once did, it is still the largest redwood industrial site in the state—and so, the world. The sawmill has self-guided tours on weekdays. Check with the Pacific Lumber Company office in Scotia for hours (Phone: 707-764-2222).

Nearby **Fortuna**, once called Slide, announces itself as "The Friendly City." I have no reason to dispute the claim after two visits to its downtown shopping district (serving a population of about 8,000) and its centrally located Rohner Park. The former Northwestern Pacific Depot has been turned into a museum of regional antiques, but its limited hours have caused me to walk around the adjacent park and its extensive flower gardens instead. (The city has an attractive Chamber of Commerce headquarters at 735 Fourteenth Street, which offers advice on local accommodations and other visitor information.) Just south of Fortuna's downtown area, Route 36 leads east from 101 into the middle of Humboldt County. Pass through the small towns of Hydesville and Carlotta, pay attention to the heavy lumber-truck traffic, and you reach a less-visited redwoods preserve, Grizzly Creek Redwoods State Park.

An exit at **Fernbridge** as you drive north on 101—three miles from Fortuna—is recommended in order to view and cross the graceful bridge that spans the Eel. It is three-quarters-of-a-century old and looks good for another century or more. Horse-drawn wagons hauled the 19,500 barrels of concrete required to build this imposing structure, whose series of arches make it an architectural beauty. Since it was built when buggies and wagons were of modest size, the two lanes seem narrow indeed as you drive the 2,500-foot span.

Beyond the bridge on Route 1, **Ferndale** is self-proclaimed as "The Victorian Village," and it does have enough examples of Victorian architecture in Northern California to satisfy most sightseers. The ornate houses and buildings were known locally as "Butterfat Palaces" because of the town's dependence on nearby dairy farms. The town's historic section is a touch heavy with landmark Victorianism, but the variety of buildings and churches dating back to the late 1800s reflects the unusual eth-

The concrete for this massive, 2,500-foot span at Fernbridge—a crossing of the Eel designed for centuries—was poured more than seventy years ago.

nic mix of the early residents: a Gothic Revival Lutheran church, a Portuguese Hall, a Queen Anne-style gingerbread mansion, an Italianate Masonic Temple, a stick-style Catholic rectory. Main Street has shops enough for strollers and a choice of Victorian inn accommodations.

Ferndale is a junction for routes to the coast. By taking the Mattole Road south from the village through Capetown, you reach the coast just below Cape Mendocino and follow it closely until the road turns inland at Petrolia. Here it is a short run along the river on Lighthouse Road to the beach. The trail past Punta Gorda to the beach below the King Range can be picked up at this point. The hike south to Shelter Cove is 24 miles. By continuing on the Mattole Road out of Petrolia it is possible to complete a loop back through Humboldt Redwoods State Park. Beyond Honeydew, the Mattole Road becomes the Bull Creek Flats Road, which ends at Highway 101.

Eureka and Arcata

Only 12 miles separate the melodically named Loleta from the discordant-sounding city of Eureka. Loleta—Indian name for pleasant place at the end of the water—was once Swauger's Station; Eureka has been Eureka since its discovery on Humboldt Bay.

Fortunately, Eureka is far more appealing than its name. As for Loleta, it is worth a stop as you drive north if only for a visit to the cheese factory in this tiny dairy community. And Loleta Drive connects with Cannibal Road, a short, straight line to the Eel River delta. There is easy fishing access at Crab County Park, an appropriate place to say farewell to the Eel, a steady companion for the traveler in northern Mendocino and southern Humboldt counties.

Eureka, with a population over 25,000, is the largest California city north of Sacramento. As you enter, Highway 101

They no longer build train depots like this one that once served the Northwestern Railroad and is now a museum in Fortuna.

becomes Broadway, one-way-only signs decorate block corners, industries, rail- and shipyards dominate to the left toward the bay, and residential streets, stores, small parks and schools spread mazelike in the other direction. It looks, on first acquaintance, like your typical small-size city. But Eureka eventually unfolds as a provocative—and attractive—town, with old maritime haunts and habits and with new renovators and young creative people who have found stimulation at the north coastal port. City planners and road builders, who not long ago were anxious to bypass the declining waterfront, with its old warehouses, saloons and seamen's boarding houses, are now part of the energetic push to preserve Old Town Eureka. The results are to the city's and its visitors' benefit.

A fairly new plaque in Old Town, next to Ramone's Opera Alley Cafe, explains that Eureka is a Greek expression and a popular mining term meaning "I have found it!" The expression is attributed to the Greek mathematician Archimedes, who discovered how, by specific gravity, to determine the proportion of base metal in Hiero's crown. Town founder James Ryan supposedly echoed Archimedes' shout of joy when he sailed his boat through the narrow channel and into the tidal waters of Humboldt Bay. I have trouble imagining how this exclamation got from ship to shore and into the legal charter in 1850. But better Eureka than Ryansville.

With neither outside warning nor planning on my part, I first went to Eureka on the brink of the annual Rhododendron Festival. I wasn't thinking rhododendrons at the time, although I had been admiring them from a distance and knew that they thrived in the moderate, moist coastal climate. The highway banners announcing the festival—"the 18th Annual"—encouraged me to stop at the Chamber of Commerce office on Broadway and find out what I might encounter.

I learned that I could get a free education on the care and development of rhododendrons at a local nursery, where 4,000 of the plants (comprising 1,300 varieties) were on display. I could run a minimarathon; enter a hole-in-one contest; attend a library book sale; taste Joe Pastori's sauce at an all-you-can-eat spaghetti feed; go to a fashion show, art show or Bach concert; watch a rhododendron stockcar race and, of course, a parade, which was conveniently scheduled to pass in front of the Eureka Inn, where I was staying.

The major activities of the festival are held over the last weekend in April and the first in May. Before and during it, I became increasingly conscious of the number of greetings I received—on the street, in restaurants, at the marina. I decided that almost everyone in Eureka knew one another and that I looked and walked unlike a Eurekan. "Oh, you're here for the festival!" they said. It was best to agree and not admit that I had blundered among the rhododendrons while trying to get some sort of fix on their town.

Eureka may be compared with Oakland in the sense that it developed inland from an enclosed bay, the second largest in the state. Humboldt Bay, shielded from the Pacific by two long, sandy peninsulas, was discovered by a Russian-American Fur Company ship working the northern coast for sea otters in the early part of the nineteenth century. It was named for the German naturalist-traveler Baron Alexander Humboldt, who died at the age of 90 in 1859. The bay's entrance is a narrow one and was a tricky passage until dredging and rock jetties were used. The waters spread north to form the wider Arcata Bay and its tidal sloughs, mudflats and marshlands. Although shipping and fishing are not what they were earlier in the century, Eureka still looks and feels like a mariner's town.

Off First Street in renovated **Old Town**, part of the fishing fleet that has supplied much of California's retail tonnage is tied up at the basin. At Woodley Island, just north in the bay, the marina has more than 225 boat slips. South of the main section of town and facing the bay's entrance, King Salmon, a small fishing community, has boat charters and boat-launching facilities, and nearby Fields Landing is a deep-sea port where the large freight-carrying ships are watched by the locals fishing off the docks. King Salmon is beyond the Pacific Gas & Electric Power Plant by Highway 101; Fields Landing at the end of Railroad Avenue, a few blocks to the south.

One early morning I walked down by Old Town's First Street Food Co-Op and Eureka Fisheries to dockside, where the *Mar Lar 583326*, the *Mari 242264* and the *Buddha 533330* were moored, moving and squeaking quietly. Fishing boats without a mission, at least on this gray morning. From one of the lighted cabins the sputter of a radio cut the silence and a voice said, "What you doing?"

"Just sitting here," came the answer.

"What time is it?"

"About five past seven."

"I was thinking coffee. . . ."

"Yea, I just started some. Come around."

It was, I assumed, a normal ship-to-ship exchange between two temporarily unemployed fishermen. Their disengaged voices contrasted with the cadenced, amplified sound that came from somewhere out in the bay, a coach exhorting her crew to greater efforts. I walked the dock far enough to catch sight of the coach's powerboat following an eight-oared shell—probably from the nearby state university—as it beat across the smooth water. While the fishing fleet idled, the rowing crew was up at dawn, pulling toward its training goal.

The salmon fleet had been stilled by a controversial 1985 ban on fishing from Point Delgada (Shelter Cove) into southern Oregon, the first time such a restriction had been placed on the commercial North Coast fleet. (The ban did not apply to sports fishermen, who are under a two-fish limit.) The decision by the Pacific Fishery Management Council was taken in an effort to rebuild the chinook salmon population in Oregon's Klamath River, whose spawning run has seriously declined. Some of the North Coast fishing boats moved south to Bodega Bay, but many others decided to ride out the bad times in home port, watching the seagulls and the drag boats go out to work the ocean bottom.

At the expansive Woodley Island Marina, which has a sidewalk running the length of the basin, I encountered a local pier walker who pointed out some of the boats for sale. The *Jo Linda,* a big, iron-hulled fish-processing ship, had recently been purchased by a doctor. The *Kimberly Michelle,* a 63-foot dragger and shrimper, could be mine for $250,000. The *Linda Ellen,* the *Jimmie Rose,* a northern troller and *Frances E,* designed for crabbing, were up for sale. I was glad to see that the freshly and gaudily painted *Last Chance* was not. A look across the forest of masts and rigging suggested that many local salmon trollers had given up for the season.

Woodley Island, which is part wildlife preserve, is reached by taking Route 235, at the end of R Street off 101. The bridge connection crosses the largest island in the bay, Indian Island, which looms heavily in accounts of the early settlement of the area. Indians occupied the island then and used it as a base for fishing and hunting expeditions. On a February night in 1860, when the hunters were away, a group of whites attacked the village, killing the remaining occupants—women, children, the old. The slaughter raised the already high stakes of revenge

The fishing fleet, stilled by coastal salmon fishing restrictions, waits in a Eureka marina in Humboldt Bay.

between the newcomers and the Indians. Young Bret Harte, working briefly for the newspaper in Uniontown, as neighboring Arcata was known then, published reports condemning the white assault. The reaction was such that he saw fit to leave town.

The bridge past Indian Island reaches the long sand spit that separates Humboldt and Arcata bays from the ocean. Turn left at the end of the bridge and the small town of **Samoa** is situated hard against the gates of the Louisiana-Pacific plywood mill, whose tall stacks dominate the skyline to the south. When I stopped at the Samoa Store for supplies and asked if it was still mostly a company town, the answer was, "Hell, yes. They own the houses, the streets, store, gas station—the works!"

To outsiders, Samoa—the name was borrowed from the Pacific island chain—is known for the "last surviving cookhouse in the West." The cookhouse was, of course, where it was at in the logging camps, the place where the lumbermen who worked dawn-to-dusk hours felling giant redwoods sat down at oilcloth-covered or bare tables and ate those gargantuan breakfasts and dinners. That lumbercamp style is preserved—long cookhouse, long tables and all—at the **Samoa Cookhouse**, popular with families, banquet-goers and diners with hearty appetites. The tables and unmatched chairs seat 12, the napkins are stuffed in coffee cans, bean salads and dressings are on hand. The waitress brings fresh bread and too much soup before you can decide whether you will have the roast beef, ribs or fried chicken. The loggers of old surely did not have such a wide choice. The Samoa slogan says that it is "not a restaurant—this is where you come to eat."

But while most cars and recreation vehicles are heading for the Cookhouse parking lot, you may choose to drive down the New Navy Base Road to Samoa Road and explore the beach opposite the town of Fair Haven, where the heavy cruiser *USS Milwaukee* went aground disastrously in 1917. Near the end of the narrow peninsula are the Eureka Airport and the Humboldt Bay Coast Guard Station. Eureka can be viewed across the bay and placed in maritime perspective. The scene also includes a mixture of white cloud emissions from the Simpson Paper Company's Humboldt Pulp Mill with the swirls of fog that come and go from the near ocean.

Follow the New Navy Base Road in the opposite direction and it leads to the Arcata Bay settlement of Manila (named for the

Its claim to fame is "the last surviving cookhouse in the West"—that and the gargantuan meals it still serves customers in Samoa.

capital of the Philippines), where a community park fronts the water. The road merges with Highway 255 at the north side of the bay and gives access to Arcata Marsh, which serves as a large filter for the city of Arcata's wastewater purifying system; the marsh is the location of a wildlife preserve, a rewarding bird-watching area of some 60 acres.

Arcata, a city of about 13,000 and the second largest in the county, was laid out around a statued old plaza. Although 101 cuts a swath through it, the city has a pleasant cohesion in appearance. A well-kept municipal ballpark adjacent to the highway is busy with games, day and night. The semi-pro Humboldt Crabs play a 52-game schedule here. Across 101 the hillside campus of Humboldt State University looks out over the city. It is the northernmost campus and has the smallest enrollment (about 7,600) of all the California state universities. The curriculum is best known for courses in forestry, oceanography and range, watershed and wildlife management. I made a self-conducted tour of the college walks, pausing to admire the old stucco buildings and the abundance of rhododendrons and azaleas in bloom. The sounds of cheering drew me to the dark green stands of Redwood Bowl, "Home of the Lumberjacks," where an interscholastic track meet was in noisy progress. It was an ideal outdoor setting for some intense schoolboy and schoolgirl athletic endeavor. Beyond the campus stadium Redwood Park— playgrounds and trails—and the Arcata Community Forest are popular with local picnic groups, hikers and joggers. Arcata claims to be the only city with its own commercial forest, 570 redwood acres that are occasionally thinned for the lumber market. At the edge of the forest, on the creeksite of a sawmill, is Jolly Giant Commons, the residence halls of Humboldt State.

Eureka is six miles from Arcata by the interior Highway 101, a quick passage if fog does not clamp down on the flatlands. Early morning fog was once an invitation for me to walk from the Eureka Inn, at 7th and F Streets past empty old waterfront buildings, to **Lazio's Restaurant** at the foot of C Street. The restaurant, one of the most recommended on the North Coast, is next to the old Lazio Fish Company, a familiar name in the business of catching and selling fish. It was shortly before the restaurant's daily opening—7:00 A.M.—so I watched a pair of trucks loading at the wholesale side of Lazio's and checked the venerable tour boat *Madaket* tied up nearby. Humboldt Bay harbor cruises leave here periodically each afternoon, with a final cocktail cruise at 5:30. They are a good, inexpensive ($4 for adults) way of finding out why this location on the bay deserved a happy shout of discovery.

Lazio's waterfront appearance is maintained within by use of heavy wood, nautical ropes at the windows, a ship's wheel and fish trophies. It attracts a good breakfast turnout and gets increasingly busy through lunch and dinner. If you are eager for an omelette at breakfast, you can make a choice among 26 combinations, ranging from such quiet wakeup alarms as plain old crabmeat to bell pepper, kielbasa or 100-mile-an-hour chili.

Winds that whip across the narrow peninsula in Humboldt Bay have leaned these trees in a Eureka sort of way.

That morning I went for eggs, sausage, fresh bran muffins and a touch of orange and strawberry on the side. The fish dishes at dinner are excellent. Recommended are baked stuffed sole (shrimp, green onions, egg sauce), salmon en brochette, West Coast snapper. (The latter is $7.95, the hearty Humboldt Bay shore dinner, $13.50.)

Lazio's is a logical starting or finishing point for a walk through **Old Town Eureka**, the restored early commercial area north of 4th Street that features shipfitters, liveries and shipping companies. Many of the old buildings on sloping 2nd Street, for years abandoned and vulnerable to removal, are occupied by shops, galleries and artisans' quarters. These enterprises and the cobblestone pavements and vintage street lamps are remindful of other civil waterfront restorations, but Eureka boasts a centerpiece of preservation all its own. The ornamented, gabled, turreted **Carson Mansion** broods above Old Town, as extreme and compelling an example of Victorian Gothic architecture as New York City's Chrysler Building is of art deco. For every visitor who looks up at this wondrous residential pile—all green and dull cream—and is astonished, repelled or delighted, there are many more who react to images of it. The mansion is one of the most photographed and sketched buildings in Northern California.

Lumberman William Carson had this house built above his redwood mills in 1885, and although some of the decorative appointments came from the East Coast, his own millhands pieced it together like so many kitchen helpers producing an anniversary cake fit for a king. It is now the headquarters of a private club. Travelers must remain content with the belief that some places are best experienced from the outside looking in.

The Carson Mansion reigns gaudily over many lesser examples of Victorian construction in Eureka. Across the street the house that William Carson built as a wedding gift for his son in 1889 boasts a gift shop. The Carter House, at the nearby corner of 3rd and L Streets, is a bed & breakfast inn and art gallery; it is a recreation of an 1884 structure in San Francisco designed by Samuel and Catherine Newsome. Scattered through the older parts of Eureka are Queen Anne cottages, octagons, Italianate designs, compact Victorian homes. The Chamber of Commerce provides a detailed listing of addresses, with architectural highlights of many houses. The **Clarke Memorial Museum**, 3rd and E Streets, contains a Victorian exhibit as well as maritime objects. It is open Tuesday through Saturday but closed in April.

On a stroll from the Carson Mansion down 2nd Street, and in need of a beer to put things in perspective again, I turned into the new **Waterfront Bar & Grill** in a renovated corner building at 1st and F Streets. The luncheon options appealed: oyster shooters were $1, the oyster stew $3.75, and the bar itself was wide and solid enough for pleasant drinking and eating. There is more new Old Town at the expanded **Eagle House Inn**, 2nd and C Streets, whose **Buon Gusto**, one of its two restaurants, dates to 1888. **Sergio's** Pasta House, across the street, attracts hungry crowds. For sourdough muffins and a range of breakfast possibilities, try the **Muffin Hatchery**, 3rd and E Streets. The **Eureka Seafood Grotto**, 6th and Broadway, open from late morning until 10:00 P.M., has fresh-catch meals and a retail sales counter.

The **Eureka Inn**, a state historical landmark, occupies a large block between 7th and F Streets, as it has since 1922. Half-timbered, Tudor-styled, it has the presence of a huge, out-of-place chalet. There are 110 guest rooms, a cavernous, chandeliered lobby with a 20-foot ceiling and constant traffic, as people hurry through it on their way to meetings or banquets in the public rooms. For all of its size and web of long hallways, it is a cheerful—and most convenient—hostelry. Room rates range from $46 to $64 (Phone 707-442-6441). Among the several motels in the downtown area, the **Red Lion Motor Inn** on 4th Street has 180 units at overnight rates from $49 to $79.

. . .

After experiencing contemporary Eureka and renewed Old Town Eureka, I found it an appropriate time to visit the high plateau site of **Fort Humboldt**, established by the U.S. Army in 1853 to protect settlers in the bay area from Indian raids. The commander Lt. Colonel Robert Buchanan chose a blufftop overlooking the bayside settlement of Bucksport. (It is reached from Highway 101 by taking the Highland Avenue Exit at the south end of the city; Bucksport still edges the bay across the railroad tracks.) When it was completed the following year, the fort had a dozen or more buildings surrounding a parade ground open at the side facing the Pacific.

Fort Humboldt's garrison was not called on to repel fiery assaults by the local tribes; rather, the soldiers were mostly involved in settling skirmishes and disputes as settlers repeatedly took Indian matters into their own hands. It wasn't until a series of treaties was made in the 1860s that white-Indian antagonism declined. Fort Humboldt was one of the most isolated of military posts. Boredom and loneliness were major enemies. One of that early contingent who suffered from the isolation was an infantry captain named Ulysses S. Grant, who, according to local storytellers, took long, solo horseback rides by day and drank in town-founder James Ryan's saloon by night. In an 1854 letter to his wife, whom he had not seen for two years,

The extravagant taste and hopes of redwood lumber baron William Carson left this magnificent pile for all Eureka visitors to see.

officer Grant commented, "You do not know how forsaken I feel here!" Soon after, Grant decided to forsake an army career and return east. Troops were withdrawn from Fort Humboldt beginning in 1866, and four years later it was abandoned. Only one of the original buildings was standing when the state acquired the property for a park in the 1950s. Plans call for the eventual reconstruction of the original garrison.

Fort Humboldt State Historic Park does have in place a permanent outdoor logging display, one that provides visitors with a concise look at the tools and methods used in the timber industry from the late nineteenth century on. A small museum is crammed with double-bit axes, springboards, Humboldt crosscut saws, old logging camp photographs—reminders that "bringing down the giant redwoods took strength, stamina . . . lots of tools." A self-employed logger's reconstructed cabin stands here and near it are redwood stumps, some six feet in diameter, examples of the challenge men faced in the high forests.

The park's most impressive displays are the old locomotive log haulers and the steam-powered "donkeys," first used in the early 1880s to bring fallen logs out by a system of overhead lines and pulleys—work that animals previously did. In the locomotive shed are the rugged little iron Andersonia of the Bear Harbor and Eel River Railroad, and the locomotive, Falk, which hauled logs to the Falk Mill until 1903.

The annual logging celebration known as Donkey Days takes place at the park during the Rhododendron Festival. Logging competitions—bucking duels, axe throwing, log rolling—are on the schedule. Rides are available on passenger cars hauled by the Bear Harbor Locomotive No. 1 along a narrow-gauge track. Perhaps only in Eureka can you admire one contestant's artistic arrangement of home-grown rhododendrons and a man's uncanny ability to throw a logging axe—all on the same late April day that was first enclosed by heavy sea fog and then opened into lovely spring sunshine.

ACKNOWLEDGMENTS

Among the printed sources I found useful in preparing this book, I would like to mention the following in the hope that the visitor to Northern California will also find them pertinent and informative.

Books: *Americans and the California Dream, 1850–1915,* by Kevin Starr; *California Coastal Access Guide* by the California Coastal Commission; *Cash Crop: An American Dream* by Ray Raphael; *Memories and Anecdotes of Early Days in Calistoga* by I. C. Adams; *Mendocino County Remembered, an Oral History* by Mendocino County Historical Society; *The Penguin Book of the American West* by David Lavender; *The Pocket Encyclopedia of California Wines* by Bob Thompson; *Robert Mondavi of the Napa Valley* by Cyril Ray; *The Silverado Squatters* by Robert Louis Stevenson; *The Valley of the Moon* by Jack London; *The WPA Guide to California: The Federal Writers' Project* (Pantheon edition, 1984; originally published in 1939).

Newspapers and Periodicals: *Anderson Valley Advertiser; Fort Bragg Advocate News; The Humboldt Beacon;* Late Harvest, 1984, California Indigenous Arts Organization; *The Mendocino Beacon; The Napa Register; The Santa Rosa Press Democrat; The Redwood Record; Ridge Review; St. Helena Star; San Francisco Chronicle; Sonoma Index-Tribune; Ukiah Daily Journal; The Weekly Calistogan; Wine Maps/The Wine Spectator.*

Also Jim Tarbell and Judy Tarbell of The Black Bear Press in Mendocino.

INDEX

ABOUT THE AUTHOR

JACK NEWCOMBE is the author of several works of fiction and nonfiction. A native of Vermont, he attended the University of Missouri, Pomona College and the American University at Biarritz before graduating from Brown University. He worked at *Life* magazine from 1955 to 1972 as a writer, editor and bureau chief in London and Washington, and enjoyed a four-year tenure as executive editor of Book-of-the-Month Club. His most recent book is the novel *In Search of Billy Cole* (Arbor House, 1984).